s a man who knows us both said, "Payne is be___ ___ than
ages. He has a bigger vocabulary. He knows ___ pe
understands more, works harder. He writes a ___ ub
all him to death to realize that his books are pedestrian and
lesser works go on and on. His reviews always betray his xxx
man they do about you, but that's all right, because he's a mu
you are. It's only his books that are inferior." That was the
I think it's a matter of morality. I think that whenever a man
st he ought to disqualify himself from passing judgment on th
e worked diligently in politics to enforce this rule, and I j
lators and critics accp ding to the nicety with which they obe
lification. The hood ones do it invariably; the poor ones do
bout Robert Payne, I could not conceivably agree to write a r
rable books covering the same ground I have covered; the prin
i would allow me to do so. I am disappointed that he would no
am sorry that Iberia has been an embarrassment to the Spanis
l to ban it outright but others have seen that it is theprinci
in bring with them. So a kind of gray silence has settled up
blicly banned, but neither is it publicly available. I under
s copies he is quietly visited by the police and advised that
t display them. So he keeps them hidden and quietly disposes
tly failing to order more. Above all else, I prize acceptance
his is not surprising, and as a matter of fact I judge it to
h government ought to do. The book contains many things diff
rd to explain, and it may be best to shunt the whole problem
old several times that a Spamish version will be printed if I
ed by the censor, and always I have said, "Go ahead." This h
s who argue, "You should resist them to the death." I rather
ons the book might do some good in wider circulation througho
r put to you, you can assure the questioner that I have agree
at it will forthcoming whenever the censor and I can get toge
y position on this is simple: the original still stands

Following the summer of '59 with Ava Gardner's naked brown legs draped over the back of that white sofa, and after that peeing contest at three in the morning with Ernest Hemingway on the Malaga Beach, what still wet-behind-the-ears gringo in Spain could be expected to become too excited at the idea in the Spring of '61 of meeting James A. Michener?

If Michener could have read my thoughts before he had come to John Fulton's studio that evening, he might have said upon shaking my hand, "Just remember, sonny. You aren't as smart as you think you are."

ROBERT VAVRA

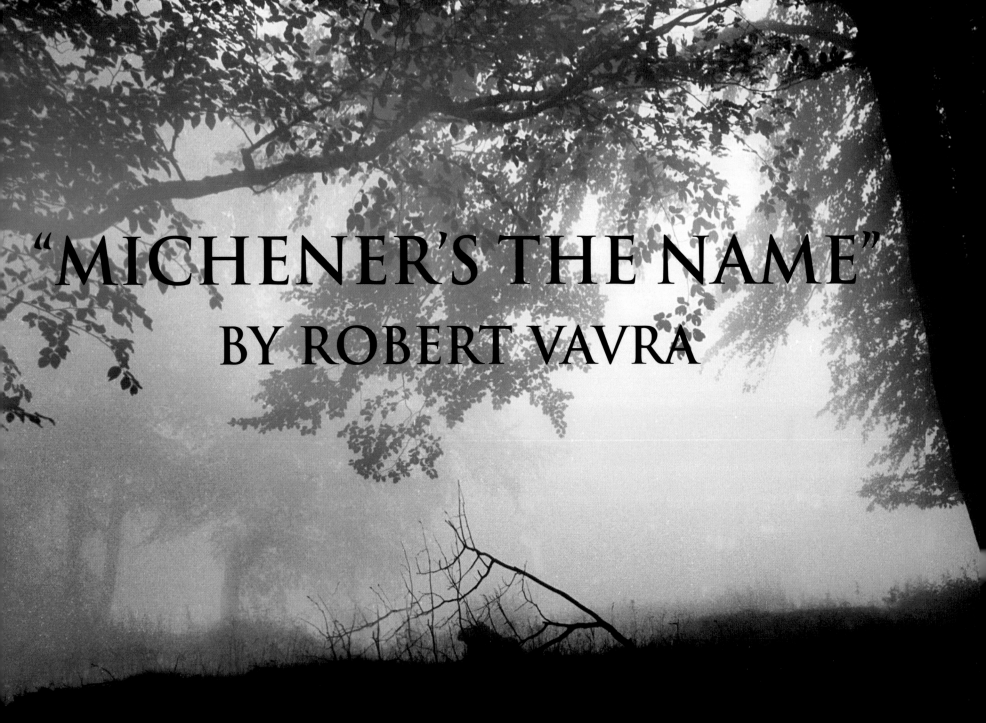

"MICHENER'S THE NAME"
BY ROBERT VAVRA

PARA MARTHA, CON TODO CORAZON,
ESTE LIBRO ES PARA TÍ.

Published by the University Press of Colorado
5589 Arapahoe Avenue, Suite 206C
Boulder, Colorado 80303

Printed in Hong Kong

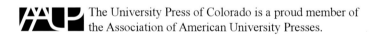 The University Press of Colorado is a proud member of
the Association of American University Presses.

The University Press of Colorado is a cooperative publishing enterprise supported, in part, by Adams State College,
Colorado State University, Fort Lewis College, Mesa State College, Metropolitan State College of Denver, University of
Colorado, University of Northern Colorado, and Western State College of Colorado.

Library of Congress Control Number: 2006050129

First Edition   1   2   3   4   5   6   7   8   9   10

DESIGNED BY ROBERT VAVRA www.robertvavra.com

All photographs in this book are by the author with the exception
of those in which he appears on p.1, p. 200, p.201, and p. 202

Printed in Hong Kong by: South Seas International Press Ltd.
3/F., Yip Cheung Centre, 10 Fung Yip Street, Chaiwan, Hong Kong
books@ssip.com.hk   Fax: (852) 2558 1473

TABLE OF CONTENTS

"Michener's the name. He just introduced himself like that," said John Fulton, shrugging his shoulders. "And he asked if I were the American bullfighter from Philadelphia. He'd seen my picture in the *Bulletin*."

"Yeah. But even then you didn't know who he was," chided Jerry Boyd.

It was early March of 1961 and I was sitting in John Fulton's studio apartment on a narrow side street a half block from the cathedral in Sevilla. John, who later became the first and only American promoted and confirmed in Spain to bullfighting's highest professional rank, *matador de toros*, was then a struggling novice who also painted and supported himself with his artwork. Jerry Boyd had once tried his hand at bullfighting in Mexico and was in Sevilla both as a writer and on his honeymoon. Twenty-six years old, I had been in Andalucía for almost two years trying to produce a book on the life of the fighting bull. Like other struggling artists who passed through Sevilla, I, along with Ileene Martin, a friend from California, was enjoying John Fulton's hospitality as he allowed us to share his roof.

"But I'm a slow reader," said Fulton.

"You've heard of *South Pacific* and *Sayanora*, or you saw Marlon Brando in the movie, didn't you? Christ," said Boyd, turning to Ileene Martin, "if I hadn't run back when John said goodbye, Michener'd never be coming up here for a drink this evening."

James Michener. What did that name mean to me then? I had never read one of his books. Hemingway, Thomas Wolfe, Carson McCullers and Salinger had interested me throughout college. Michener I only connected with Bloody Mary singing "Bali-Hai" in a road show production of *South Pacific* I had seen in Pasadena. He was a popular writer whose name, though it often appeared high and long on the best-seller list, had never attracted my attention enough to make me pick up one of his books. In college, when English Lit professors gave us reading lists for book reviews, *Tales of the South Pacific* was not among my choices, because World War II in the South Pacific didn't interest me, while Africa, Spain, and bullfighting did.

Hemingway! Now, that was something else. In the late fifties he was the great white-bearded god of literature and manhood to me and thousands of other Americans. I remember listening enraptured, thinking who could ever be so lucky, as an English professor at USC told of a late afternoon experience in Cuba. Walking a deserted beach, he had seen a lone figure sitting on the end of a pier that jutted into turquoise water. Our professor had walked out onto the pier, and for the next half hour found himself speaking with and listening to Ernest Hemingway. In those days, if someone had asked me about a popular writer called Michener–or was it Mitchener?–I would have wondered how anyone could have been interested in him and World War II and the South Pacific when there was Ernest Hemingway, bullfights, Ava Gardner and Spain.

In August of 1959, John Fulton and I were introduced to Hemingway at the Malaga fair where we met him at the Miramar Hotel bar after almost every bullfight. Following one corrida, we went to a small restaurant called Antonio Martin on the Malaga Bay, where Hemingway was seated at the head of the table, John and I on either side of him. And there, from eleven that night until three the following morning, we had an interested, sincere Ernest Hemingway practically all to ourselves. We talked about Africa and bullfights and about his books and the movies that had been made from them. It pleased me to know that he thought highly of the job Robert Preston had done in the Zoltan Korda film, *The Macomber Affair*. When he spoke about his friends and enemies, he cautioned us that this "table talk" couldn't be repeated. At three in the morning, as we left the table on the sand, Hemingway, John and I lingered while the others went ahead, and because the wine had stimulated our bladders and our school-boy American humors, we had a peeing contest against a phone pole on the beach. Hemingway won it as easily as he had won us over that evening.

Ernest Hemingway followed by Ava Gardner in the summer of '59. That was stiff competition in the spring of '61 for Michener or any other writer who hasn't spent a lifetime working on his public image. During that "Dangerous Summer," as Hemingway called it, John Fulton and I had traveled from bull fair to bull fair, with two glamorous, beautiful, wealthy and older-by-fifteen-years-than-we English women. It was exciting, after having hung out most of my life at Bob's Big Boy Drive-in in Glendale, California, to come to Madrid, lose my virginity (with a green-eyed divorcee who was ten years my senior), have my first gin and tonic at the Jockey Club, and to one evening arrive early for a party at a luxurious Madrid penthouse to find myself alone with the woman of my dreams. That introduction couldn't have been more romantic had it appeared one Saturday night on the silver screen of the Alex Theatre in Glendale. Soft music was playing as a butler ushered me into a split-level room decorated with tropical plants,

Continued on page 140

The rain fell harder as Michener, Fulton and I reached the car, mud oozing around its smoothly worn tires. Completely soaked, we pushed the old Ford for another hundred yards until our footing became firmer.

ROBERT VAVRA

*The matador suddenly cried, "Look," and off to our left, rising
from the reeds and thistles like an apparition, loomed a gray bull, his*

The Concha y Sierra ranch foreman, Diego, liked Jim and convinced him to climb onto the old horse Gorrión. It was the only time I ever saw Michener in the saddle.

Mari and I are very happy in our home in Bucks County. It's one of the grand parts of America. We like it in all seasons, especially when we are snowed in in winter, which we are almost every year. We travel only when invitations build up of such ravishing enticement that we can't say no. In recent years the invitations to do creative things in all parts of the world have been coming in at the rate of about three a month, year in, and year out.

JAMES A. MICHENER

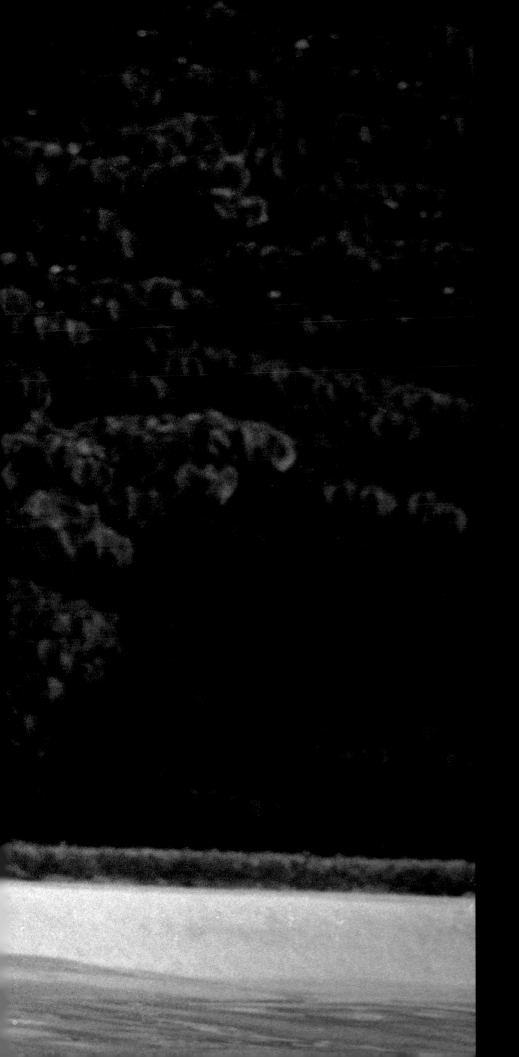

On the hill, at places known only to me, are buried eight much-loved dogs. They always came in pairs - China and Java, Burma and India. I never try to explain to people who have not had dogs how sensible human beings can love these splendid animals so much. The other reason I rarely speak of the dogs to strangers is that when they have died I have experienced a grief that could not have been exceeded had they been human beings. They were my mentors, my constant companions, my unfailing friends who always loved the hill as much as I did.

JAMES A, MICHENER

Bob, I'll focus my eyes and you focus your camera on the faces of Spain…

JAMES MICHENER

You remember that July. When I got off the plane...my first flight after the massive heart attack. That very hot day in Madrid. And I just about collapsed. And how carefully I took it in Teruel, trying to build up my strength to see how much I would be good for. And the slow gathering of confidence, even though I was so extremely thin. And then gradually getting the feel of it again, and the good drive north to Tudela.

JAMES A. MICHENER

Judging from what people tell me, I was a difficult, self-directed, hell-raising young man. I appear to have been insecure in social matters, fearfully coordinated intellectually. I got mostly straight A's and gave the impression of being unlikely ever to get it together.

JAMES A. MICHENER

I've always done all my own research. Only me. I don't read German or Russian and often have to pay for translations in those languages. But I'm not impressed when someone praises me for having done research. I had a good education. I was taught by some very good professors. It would be astonishing if I couldn't do research.

JAMES A. MICHENER

You and I persuaded the police to let me sit on the top of the post right where the bulls turned the corner, because I wanted

The last morning I went into the street itself with the fighting bulls thundering past a few inches away. Why would a man who had been so close to death only a short time before subject himself to such a risk? I think it is because one must not take death too seriously. I sensed that if I were going to survive the serious heart attack I had suffered I could do it only one of two ways: I could be a pampered cripple who had retired from life, or I could return to where I was before and take every risk I had ever taken. Pamplona was the test, and when the bulls thundered past and I felt only a surge of normal excitement, I knew that I was free to resume whatever life I had enjoyed in the past.

JAMES A. MICHENER

Fun? James Michener. Matt Carney. Oliver Nicholls. This picture speaks for itself.

ROBERT VAVRA

"In the twenty years I worked for him I never saw him laugh like in this photograph," Debbie Brothers said to me.

"He had just been in the street with the bulls," I told her. After his recent heart attack he seemed to be as joyful as the young people with whom he danced and joked and laughed in celebration of being alive.

ROBERT VAVRA

Average citizens hate artists. I've warned you and Fulton about that before, but the hate wells up to the surface only in times of stress. Throughout my professional life I have received a constant trickle of hate mail, most of it unsigned but from my neighbors, and it's done me a lot more good than harm, because it reminds me of what we talked about one other time. It is really us against them. They need us to comment on their lives or to arrange the evidence they see in fresh and compelling ways, but they hate us at the same time. I have never whined about this, because I think it's not a bad posture to be in. It helps keep us clean. It helps keep us from kidding ourselves as to the true state of affairs. I have no complaints.

JAMES A. MICHENER

...Michener understood as well as possible how much of my life was tied up in becoming a full matador...when I ran into some bad luck in Madrid as a novillero, *it was Jim's voice that cut through the condemnation and confusion, giving me an arm to lean on and regain the equilibrium to continue fighting for what I believed in. When I became the only American in history to be ordained as full*

…to have the heart of a child is not a disgrace. It is an honor. A man must comport himself as a man. But it is never a reproach that he has kept a child's heart, a child's honesty, and a child's frankness and nobility.

ERNEST HEMINGWAY

At Pamplona, and especially on our picnics at Roncesvalles, Jim was more relaxed than I've ever seen him. He clowned around like the kids he was with.

The Ashcrafts and Mari held a straw mat to suggest the bullring fence, while Fulton acted the role of the bull, jabbing his horns into a laughing matador.

ROBERT VAVRA

57

I have a very warm spot in my heart for John Fulton. Any guy from South Philadelphia, six feet one inch tall, who decides at age twenty to become a matador de toros, *is so totally unhinged that there must be something glorious about him. With guts like that you don't need charm or insight, but John had them, too. I think some of the happiest days I spent in Spain were with Fulton.*

JAMES A. MICHENER

How do I feel about dying? I've had a good life. I'd done what I could. I've had a lot of failures and my share of success and what the hell could I do about it now? At this late stage. Regrets? None. Well, there are some things I'd have changed of course. But deep nagging regrets that my life has been a waste? None. It has been a good run, a lot of laughs, a lot of challenges

He belonged to the storyteller school. Like Somerset Maugham, he is a talented literary craftsman first and foremost.

NORMAN COUSINS

Bennett Cerf ran into where I was working, with that incredible photograph of the young faun (Truman Capote)…reclining languorously on a chaise lounge… "Look what some SOB sent me!"…Cerf bellowed… "What you need, Michener, is a photograph like this. An attention getter."

Tales of the South Pacific. *I was on a miserable little island listening one night as sailors and airmen bitched about the place, and it suddenly occurred to me that twenty years from that night, if they lived, they'd remember the South Pacific with a certain affection. This moved me deeply and I went for a walk in the starry night to the end of the pier. I was determined that I would write an honest account of what the islands had been like.*

JAMES A. MICHENER

Michener has two round Spanish bread rolls, one large and one small, in either hand pressed to his chest as he recites,

"There once was a woman from Nizes
With breasts of two different sizes

One was so small, it was hardly there at all
And the other was large and won prizes."

I remember when there was a good deal of talk in Spain about an American matador taking up with a black bellydancer, and on the face of it you'll have to admit that this is not an ordinary pairing. We got to talking about the interracial thing and yes, I recall I said that about the best thing I'd done in life was to marry Mari. It was pretty early for an interracial marriage, and especially to a Japanese.

My nose, if you've observed, takes a pronounced jag to the right. I've had it broken three times for speaking out of turn. I was younger then and it took me a long time to learn.

JAMES A. MICHENER

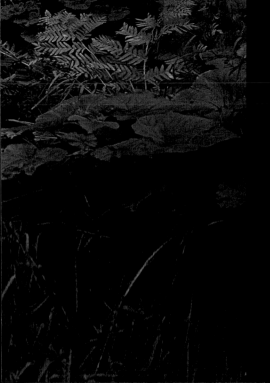

James Michener seems to me a true American classic. His enormous success has not hardened his heart but seems to have had quite the reverse effect upon him.

Surely he has touched every man, woman, and child in the United States over the decades by way of his novels...

JOYCE CAROL OATES

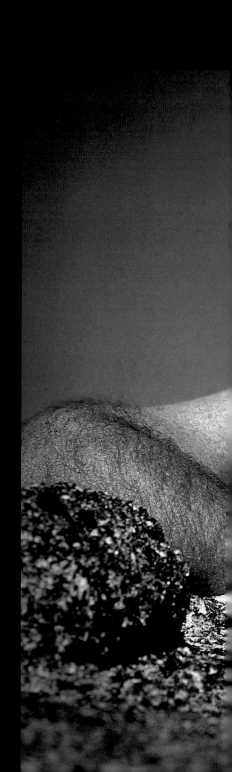

My two aunts were very conservative. When I brought a Japanese bride home, they weren't the least surprised and they took her to their hearts as if she were their own daughter. But, they were appalled that she was a Democrat. She asked Aunt Hannah, "Have you ever known a Democrat?" And Aunt Hannah said, "I think there used to be one...on the edge of town."

JAMES A. MICHENER

Why do millions of people buy James Michener's books and why does every bed lamp shine down on his newest title? Isn't it because he has spent 40 years coming back from far journeys and difficult languages, to tell us about other people's other ways of life? Other challenges and other lives survived?

RUTH GOETZ

I have never had much confidence in myself as a person, but I have felt secure within my world such as it was. Most important, I have had in my life only two or three original ideas, and they came to me before I was twenty-five. I do believe that the world has had no surprises for me, only the orderly unfolding of phenomena that spring from disorderly causes.

JAMES A. MICHENER

It was in Pamplona that I met The Drifters, *a chance encounter that would take me to Torremolinos, Morocco, and Mozambique. As with that chance meeting with John Fulton, it would lead to the writing of another book.*

JAMES A. MICHENER

I read the reviews of Lawrence of Arabia *and then saw your boy Peter in the film. He was even better than your description. I can picture you, Fulton, and O'Toole in Sevilla after a night out boozing, sitting on the curb in the rain while the cathedral bells chimed four in the morning, and O'Toole recited Dylan Thomas.*

JAMES A. MICHENER

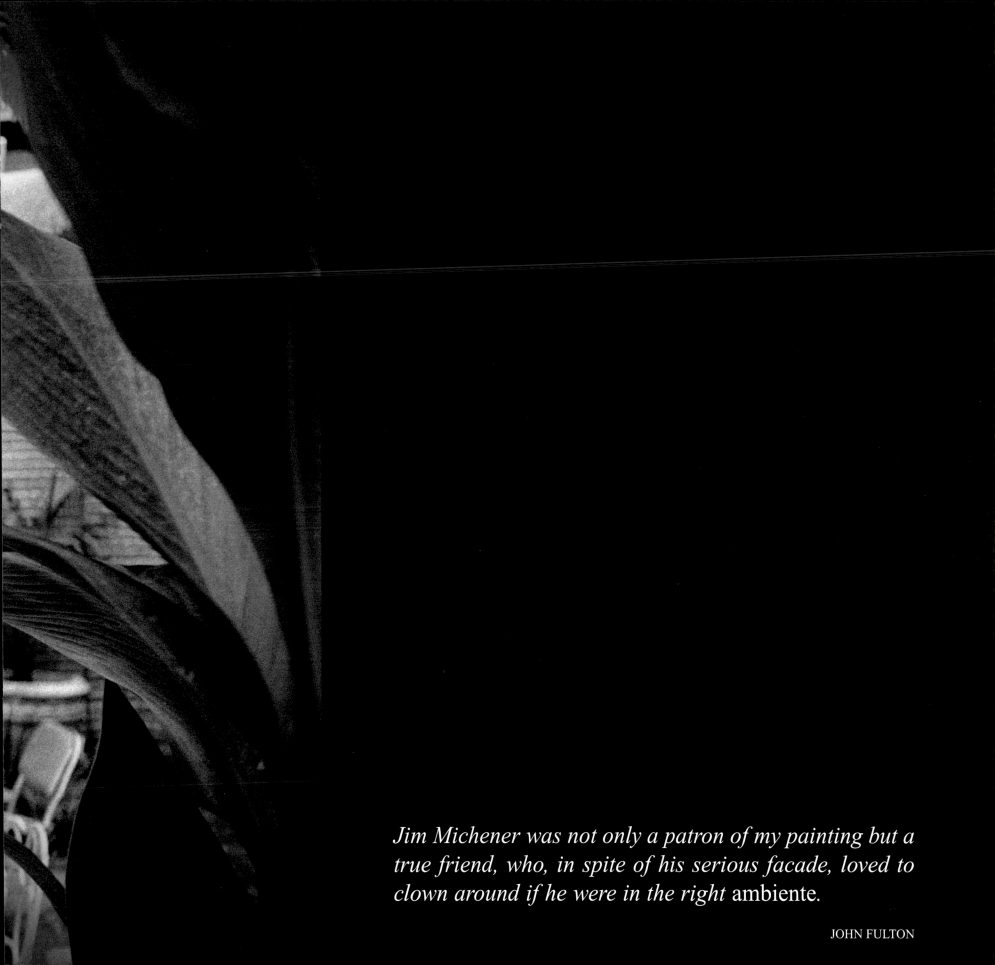

Jim Michener was not only a patron of my painting but a true friend, who, in spite of his serious facade, loved to clown around if he were in the right ambiente.

JOHN FULTON

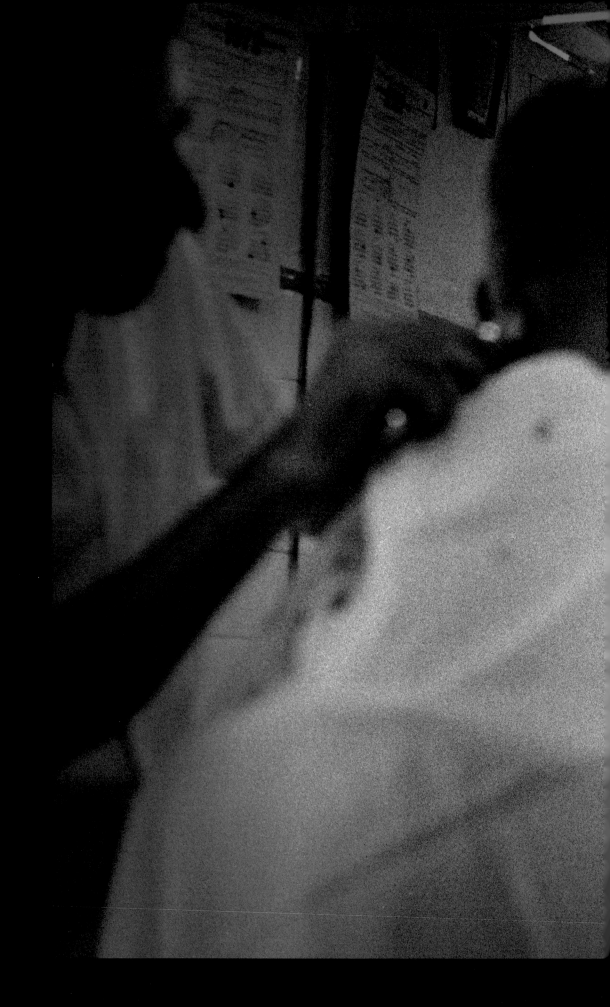

You think, "If I were starting today could I get to first base?" Pretty surely I couldn't get Tales of the South Pacific *published today. So I am not being mock-modest when I say that I have known quite a few young men who can write better than I can who have never had the breaks. Not even break one. And this can be very sobering.*

JAMES A. MICHENER

That damned hyena persists in my memory. I remember when I first walked up to him. He smelled me and discovered that I wasn't afraid, so he took my right forearm in his jaws and looked up at me with almost a wink in his eye as if to say, "Boy, could I do you in."

JAMES A. MICHENER

He has cast a wide net and touched men and women confronting prac-tical problems and looking to the written word for clues to life. He has made the word "popular" respectable, and that's a solid accomplish-ment in this slippery era.

ARTHUR MILLER

"We need a few blurbs," said my publisher. "Some names. Big Names. Literary names."

"I don't know any big names. Literary names," I protested.

Damp with perspiration of embarrassment, I sent James Michener the galleys. Also Cheever, and Malamud.

Three days later, a letter arrived from James Michener which contained a generous quote.

It was used gratefully. It helped immensely.

Ask me about James Michener.

GARSON CANON

People ask why a man who can write books the way I do dirties himself with politics. It's the other way around. I write the kinds of books I do because I've always been interested in politics.

JAMES A. MICHENER

People who have watched me work get real scared. I work like mad and refuse to be stopped by the lack of data. I deal with everything on the T.K. basis. To Kome later. The important thing is to keep your own commitment high, to be on top of the ballgame. The checking of data can come later, when the fire's gone.

During the feria *at Sevilla I heard this street singer with a guitar…I remember him as an old man but it could have been a woman. He was singing,* "Yo soy un ánima infeliz, Perdida en este mundo atormentado," *(I am a miserable spirit, Lost in this tormented world) and I jotted down the words thinking, "He speaks for anyone trying to make his way as an artist."*

JAMES A. MICHENER

112

Truest saying in our profession is that if you vaguely want to write and haven't written a complete book by age thirty-five, you never will. I was forty and I often wake up at night and shudder to think how narrowly I escaped.

JAMES A. MICHENER

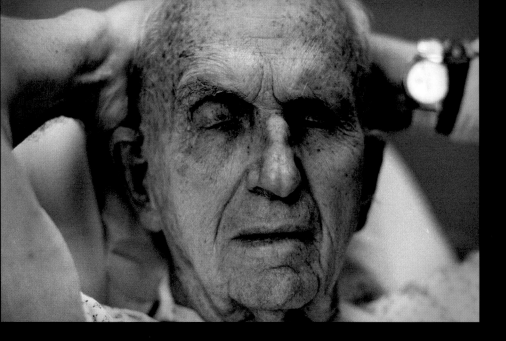

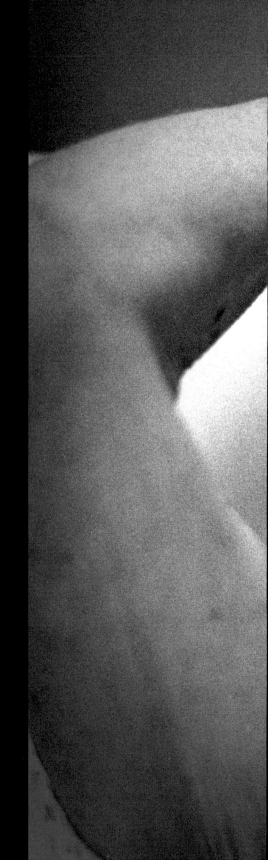

I sit for hours with Michener in the hospital. The IV in his arm is not as disturbing as the dark circles under his eyes and right carotid artery throbbing in his neck. "You know, Bob," he says, "that story of the woman at Fulton's fight in Tijuana…" His eyes close and he stops speaking. Is he dying? Should I call a nurse?

Ten minutes pass. Slowly he opens his eyes and without missing a beat, continues, "Yes, it was in Tijuana…"

ROBERT VAVRA

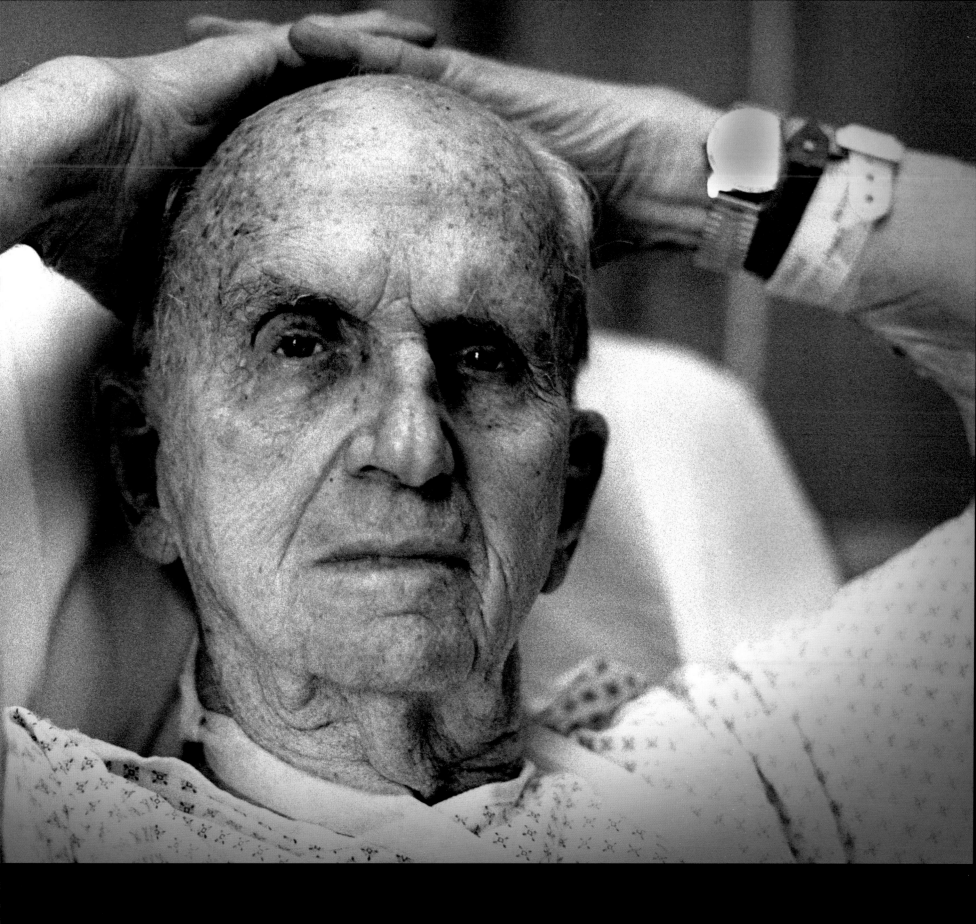

…Like me she wanted to be cremated and buried where she fell. Her grave lies under a tree with these words in Kentucky limestone:

Mari Sabuswa Michener
1920-1994
Philanthropist
Art Lover
Wife

Only now have I had the composure to report these happenings. Please accept this letter as a memory of that gallant, never-surrendering little Japanese girl…

I stand for certain things. I believe in certain values...Every time I sit down to write anything, no matter how simple, I want to hit somebody over the head with it. I want to show and illuminate and persuade and convince.

JAMES A. MICHENER

"MICHENER'S THE NAME…"

Continued from page 8

macaws and a waterfall. I stood self-consciously alone until I looked around a philo-dendron to see a lovely pair of female legs hanging over a white sofa. "Hello," I announced my presence.

"Hello." From the sofa and legs came a voice that I had heard so many times in the Alex Theatre, a voice from *The Killers*, *The Sun Also Rises*, and *The Snows of Kilimanjaro*.

Rising from the sofa, slim and clear-eyed, was Lady Brett in person. So what does a square Glendalian talk about when he finds himself alone for a half hour with Ava Gardner? She called Hemingway "Papa" and had been Luis Miguel Dominguin's *amante*, which eliminated bullfighting as a topic of conversation. The Basenji, though, was one subject about which I could converse with confidence, so while Ava Gardner stretched out so beautifully and smiled her marvelous smile back at me, I talked about African barkless dogs.

After the summer of '59 with Ava Gardner's brown legs hanging over the back of that white sofa, and following that peeing contest at three in the morning with Ernest Hemingway on the Malaga beach, what still wet-behind-the-ears gringo in Spain could be expected to become too excited at the idea, in the spring of '61, of meeting James A. Michener? If Michener could have read my thoughts before he had come to John Fulton's studio that evening, he might have said upon shaking my hand, "Just remember, sonny. You aren't as smart as you think you are."

Before meeting a famous author, it's hard not to identify him with his books and heroes. So that evening, as Ileene and I waited for Michener, even though neither of us had read one of his bestsellers, our imaginations began to picture him. Yes, the South Pacific. Michener was sure to be wearing a captain's cap cocked back on his tan fore-head. If he didn't have a beard, he was bound to have mutton chop sideburns. His pipe would be lit and he'd have a craze for rum that couldn't be satisfied. And his muscular arms, without the slightest doubt, would be decorated with real Chinese tattoos. Unlike Hemingway, Steinbeck and other authors whose faces we had seen in newspaper and magazine photographs, neither of us could ever remember having seen a mug shot of Michener, even though his new book *Hawaii* was the bestseller rage of the year.

Because those were the good old days in Sevilla, almost fifty years ago, when there were few cars in the city, the noise from the narrow street below Fulton's second-floor studio was minimal. So it was that with clarity we heard a deep voice that evening calling from under the balcony, "Fulton! Hey, John Fulton!" Ileene and I went to the window. In the fading light, barely distinguishable in the street below us, was a conservatively dressed man, maybe in his mid-fifties, with a pair of light framed spectacles on his rather bulbous nose.

"Hello," shouted Ileene, after which she looked questioningly at me, appearing to share my thoughts: "Where is the famous South Seas author with his captain's cap, beard and pipe? This must be his chauffeur? But why is he calling from the street instead of ringing the doorbell?"

"I'm Jim Michener," said the man. "Is John home?"

Just as I reached the stairway and was pulling the chain that would open the door to the street, John Fulton, Gerry Boyd and his wife also arrived and came up the stairs with their guest. Upon getting a good look at Michener in the light of the studio, I thought, and friends to whom I later introduced him had the same impression, "He looks like a god-damned school teacher!" Of medium height with powerful arms and legs and not even one tattoo, Michener's full but rounded shoulders and wide backside would have disqualified him for Tyrone Power or Jon Hall roles in South Pacific adventure films. His receding hairline, sensitive, large eyes, and Karl Malden nose, though, might have won him a missionary part.

Except for Fulton, the rest of us were nobodies, though Jerry Boyd's lovely new bride was the daughter of actor Abraham Sofaer. So there was a certain air of nervousness in the room as we found ourselves in the company of this celebrity. However, James Michener's natural manner soon put us at ease. His voice was deep and steady and he spoke with a certain slowness that made you feel everything he said had been soundly thought out and assessed. As he told us that he was researching a novel on Mexico, he would now and then put his powerful hands into a praying position, touching the ends of his fingers to his lips. Probably the most expressive part of his face–though his large eyes, magnified behind his glasses, demanded certain attention–was his mouth. Then, and over the years, I was able to determine Michener's mood from his mouth. If he was happy, his lips and the lower part of his jaw were relaxed and naturally full. If he was angry–and in all of those years I really only saw him seriously mad on three or four occasions–his lips would tense as he rigidly set his lower jaw. If he was melancholy, sad and miserable, swamped down by depression, his conversation, if he felt like speaking, never revealed his inner torment, but his mouth did, as it took a downward curve at the edges to let anyone know who could read his face that he felt perfectly awful inside. While the rest of us sucked gin and tonics, James Michener sipped on one cerveza that evening at John Fulton's place. In all the years I knew him, I only saw him mildly high a couple of times and that was on beer, a beverage that wasn't even a normal part of his diet.

After we sat around the studio for awhile, with Michener, John and Jerry doing most of the talking, Michener invited us to dinner. Being so poor those days in Sevilla, and often receiving dinner invitations from tourists who had heard of the American bullfighter and had sought him out, John, Ileene and I had a list of restaurants ready to suggest, depending on the spending power of our hosts. This was a real treat for us, especially during the springtime when the flow of tourists started south and we sat not too much unlike three Peregrine falcons waiting at the Gulf of Mexico for the songbird migrations to begin.

During the tourist high season we probably averaged four invitations a week. The rest of the time, because we were so poor, we ate all of our meals standing up at a cheap restaurant behind the post office. In winter, except when Ileene would complain, "I'm sick of standing up eating like a horse every noon and night" and would stir up a pot of noodles, tuna, mushroom soup, and cheese (which we called "noodles blubber") over the Aladdin heater, we would go for weeks, and sometimes months, never knowing what it was to feel chairs beneath our bottoms while we fed our faces. Often, in those days, I would search my trouser pockets, hopeful of finding enough of those old Spanish aluminum coins–twenty equalled a U.S. penny–to buy myself a roll and a cup of tea for breakfast. Often unsuccessful, I would have to be satisfied with a glass of hot water collected from our five-gallon electric shower tank.

So, when James Michener invited us for dinner and asked us to name the spot, our empty stomachs rumbled with delight. Even though we felt Michener must have been a wealthy man–so many of his books had been made into films–because of the conservatively square way he was dressed, his school teacher appearance, and humble manner, we didn't suggest eating at the Alfonso XIII Hotel, in its dining room of immense crystal chandeliers and elegant tables, each surrounded by at least five waiters. Instead, we named Los Corrales, a moderately-priced but nice restaurant at the beginning of the Calle Sierpes.

When we left the studio and Michener, arms behind his back, strolled along talking to Ileene, I again had the chance to appreciate the size of his hands and feet. Stepping fairly quickly along, he seemed to carry himself a bit self-consciously, bending slightly forward at the waist. The evening was warm and it felt good to be young in Sevilla, walking with friends and with a bestselling author.

Our meal at Los Corrales was well prepared and filling, and by the time it was over, Michener had won over all of us with his simple manner, his stimulating conversation, his sense of humor, and his knowledge of so many subjects. He was so well-read, so well-travelled, so interested in art, music, sports, bullfighting and Spain, all things that mutually attracted us. Though in no way was he a name dropper, the famous people who were his friends or acquaintances were also impressive to our young ears. If he was a brilliant conversationalist, he was just as good a listener. About the work that had brought him to Spain, he didn't say much, except that he was starting a novel that dealt with Mexico. In the thirty-six years that would follow, with the exception of *Iberia*, I never heard him discuss in length any of the projects he had in mind or upon which he was working. The experiences that he had while researching, he often spoke of or wrote me about, but to avoid expelling the creative energy that he was pouring into a book, he wasted few words to others about his work.

After we left Los Corrales that night, although we knew James Michener would be in Sevilla for the month that included Holy Week and the Spring Fair, I didn't expect to see him again except in casual passings. However, the following afternoon from below the studio balcony, I heard the voice from the evening before. "Fulton! Vavra!" Though I was happy to hear him, 'Why doesn't this guy use the doorbell?' I wondered.

Later that evening, I asked Michener if he would do a rough bull sketch for a collection I was making for possible end paper decorations for my book on the life of the fighting bull. His drawing, which precedes one that Jean Cocteau had done in Malaga, shows a bull with enormous horns facing a stick-figure matador who is saying, "To hell with this racket. I'm going back to tennis."

For the next week or so, Michener visited us on an almost daily basis. Often we'd just sit around the studio, talking, joined by other young foreigners who were trying to make their way in Spain. There must have then been about twenty American, British, Irish, and Australian youths hanging on in Sevilla then, most of them giving English lessons to keep alive and to pay for their flamenco dancing or guitar lessons. And, when they weren't drinking wine in the Bar Morales, many of them gathered at Fulton's place.

Among this group, listening as we expressed our hopes, dreams, and frustrations, Michener would sit in an old wicker chair, his hands folded together, index fingers to his lips. Once in a while I would glance over to find him looking at the enlargements of my black and white photographs that decorated one of the studio walls, and I sensed with some pleasure what seemed in his eyes to be more than a passing interest in my work.

Almost from the beginning, James Michener made it clear that you had to be completely on the up and up with him. If you weren't, he'd call you on it. He expressed interest and gave serious advice to John about his painting, and he seemed concerned with my projected book on the life of the fighting bull. He also took Ileene under his wing and had a real way with young ladies. His smile was especially wide and his eyes sparkled when he spoke to one of the girls who visited the apartment. The impression he gave was of the high school English or history teacher who felt a deep concern for his students and who was probably responsible for putting many of them onto a positive road in life. Often, though, I lamented this first impression when I'd introduce the famous writer James Michener to friends and could read the disappointment on their faces. If he had only sported just one tattoo, had a beard, or now and then wore a captain's cap, I wished at first. But later I knew that if my friends had the chance to get to know Michener, they'd probably be completely taken with him.

One afternoon, as I was sorting negatives, Michener, who had been sitting reading in the studio, put down his book and asked if I'd like to do some research for him. I could earn a little money, he said. He'd pay me one hundred and fifty dollars to provide him with some notes on Concha y Sierra, the bull ranch where I was doing most of my own work. When I realized that the information requested of me could have been gathered in two or three hours from the bullfighting books at the studio, I became aware that James Michener was trying to give me a hand in the same way he was helping John Fulton by commissioning him to do a painting. Later I was to learn that he had tried to help young people in many parts of the world by offering them simple jobs; having always worked for his own income, he felt that no good could come from gift money.

During Holy Week we saw Michener less frequently, and it was at this time that, after weeks of trying, I found a pocket edition of *Hawaii*. Before then I was sensitive that somehow in conversation he would learn I had never read one of his books. But even more than that, since I had grown to care for him, I was truly interested to see what kind of books my new friend and part-time employer wrote.

Being a self-styled naturalist, I was fascinated by the book's opening chapter–found boring by many readers–describing the formation of the island. Later, Michener told me, "If they can get through it, then I'm glad to have them aboard. The ones who complain or drop by the wayside in that chapter aren't the sort of readers who should follow through with the rest of the book anyway."

The old Chinese woman, Nyuk Tsin, became my favorite character. It seemed Michener had given her more life than anyone else in the book, which I read from cover to cover with more than casual interest. There were descriptive passages of extreme beauty that were as artfully written as anything I had ever read. Other sections impressed me as being well-written by a good writer who was more guided by a mission than by inspiration. As believable and real as Nyuk Tsin seemed, other characters, especially those toward the end of the book, seemed stiff. But, all in all, the book was an educational and enjoyable experience and I was sorry to see the last page come. It was an ideal fat summer book, the kind you could put down, knowing that in spare moments another six hundred pages of entertainment and learning lay ahead.

It amused me, never having been interested in *Hawaii*, that after finishing Michener's book my head was full of information about its history, people and agriculture. And then, the merit of James Michener's writing, if *Hawaii* was an example of it, became apparent. He was, in part, what he appeared to be–a teacher who made learning enjoyable by mixing fact and fiction together in bulky, well-written, entertaining books. For me, he brought Hawaii's foggy history to life. From that book I also learned that its author was a crusader against social, political, racial, and religious prejudice.

When Holy Week was over, we once more began to see Michener on almost a daily basis. By now he was 'Jim' or 'Mich' to us. However, even though his behavior indicated we could be ourselves in his presence, I was still insecure enough to try to keep on my toes with him, while also attempting to give the impression that I wasn't inhibited by his fame. During those two weeks between Holy Week and the fair, Fulton, Jim, and I made a number of short trips into the marshes where fighting bulls are raised along the Guadalquivir River. One afternoon I remember in particular: We had driven out among the rice fields on a dirt road, recently turned to mud by spring rains, which led to the Concha y Sierra ranch. Having forced the old Ford Consul as far as we felt we could safely go on the slippery road, either side of which was flanked by a deep canal of water, we left the car and trudged ahead on foot toward the ranch house. The late afternoon sky, shaded dove gray by an approaching storm, was billowing with fast-moving, downy white clouds pushed in from the Atlantic by a wind that also bent the rice plants and rippled water in the fields around us.

When we reached the ranch house, we were met by the old foreman, Diego, who asked if I wanted to show our guest the inside of the crumbling, unoccupied *cortijo* before we went to look at the bulls. The house, which had stood practically abandoned for a quarter of a century, was still cold and damp inside from the recent winter. As we paused now and then to look at bull paintings that were cracked with age and which hung on flaky white-washed walls, I chronicled in few words the strange family history of Concha y Sierra for Michener. I began with Fernando de la Concha y Sierra, *Sevillano* playboy, and his marriage to the young Italian dancer, Celsa Fonferde, to his early death, age forty-one, at the end of the eighteenth century, followed by his widow's scandalous affair with the famous matador El Espartero, which ended with the birth of a daughter, who was the mother of the wild boys who then ran the ranch. As I spoke, Michener seemed completely caught up in the story, for this was just the kind of family history that fascinated him and formed, or would form, the foundations of his most widely-read books, including *Hawaii*, *The Source*, *Centennial*, *Chesapeake*, *Poland*, *Alaska*, *Texas*, and *Mexico*.

Upon leaving the dampness of the house, we made our way along a trail into a field of tall green thistles where Diego told us the four-year-old bulls could be found. It was then that I learned Michener had a keen interest in animal and bird life. As the years passed, I found in his writings creatures such as the bee-eater and hoopoe, to which I had introduced him. As we walked deeper into the thistles, we were confronted by a stand of tall reeds that rose from a marsh bordering the pasture. Reaching a water trough near the edge of the marsh, we waited. The sky darkened and the wind became more intense as Jim zipped up his windbreaker and jabbed his hands deep into its pockets. John Fulton squatted down next to the trough and I stood squinting into the reeds, hopeful, since I was supposedly an authority on fighting bulls, of being the first to spot one of the immense Concha y Sierra animals. But it was Fulton who whispered that he saw movement to our left as a group of shapes, led by a gray beast whose horns took an upward swing like those in the Goya engravings, slowly filed out of the marsh and into the field. Pocket-size spiral notebook in hand, Jim began taking notes in a minute script, glancing now and then from the pad as he squinted through his glasses at the approaching herd.

Inspired by Michener's obvious interest in the animals, a thought came to mind. I was then well into my bull book, and being aware of the difficulty of finding a publisher for this study of such limited interest, it had been my idea in the summer of 1960 to make it more appealing by asking Ernest Hemingway to write its introduction. Following meetings with Hemingway in 1959 at the Malaga fair, I gratefully accepted his financial help but was unable to accept his offer of assistance with my writing. I was too broke to leave Sevilla to meet him in northern Spain and had to take a job for the summer months or face returning to America.

Since I knew Hemingway would be at the 1960 Jerez fair, I gathered some of my bull photographs and went there. I also took along a pair of binoculars, with which, as I sat in a cheap seat that afternoon on the sunny side of the ring, I scanned the shady side first row until I saw the man with the white beard. Staring through those field glasses, I was filled with sadness: Did I really have reason or the right to those feelings? Hemingway was not my close friend. I had known him only briefly, though he had been kind to me and I had liked him. His books, however (which in a way made him public property) had for years made him my idol and inspiration.

Peering through those glasses, I could only think of the saddest zoo inmate I had ever known, a polar bear at Griffith Park in Los Angeles, an old animal that would sit for hours, its white head resting on its great paws, staring into space, lost perhaps in recollection of another life, another time, a time of youth and strength and hunts and illusions that since had melted like icebergs, only to awaken caged by a worn-out body and a clouded mind. Throughout most of the *corrida*, I kept my eyes on Hemingway, and even when his young idol Ordoñez performed brilliantly, the old man showed little reaction. Once or twice he slowly raised his hands and clapped methodically, as though he were the old bear who had broken from his trance and was tiredly batting his paws together, begging for peanuts. When the fight was over, I didn't go to the hotel where the bull crowd could be found nor did I search out anyone, for the person I had wanted to speak with in Jerez so obviously could no longer be found in Spain or Africa or Cuba or anywhere. Sadly, so very sadly, I packed up my photographs and my romantic illusions and walked out into the brisk fall night to try to hitch a ride back to Sevilla.

Watching James Michener observe the bulls coming toward us made me realize that he not only had the qualities so essential to the journalist, but he had, as well, the patience and quiet manner of a naturalist. By this time Diego had saddled up the old white horse, Gorrión, and had ridden into the field to find us. Once we were sighted, he motioned for me to climb up behind him, after which we plodded out into the reeds to slowly urge several bulls toward the water trough. As we moved along, the fresh odors of blooming spring flowers, trampled grass and bull dung–all sweet to the nostrils of anyone who loves the Spanish countryside–and of Diego's sour sweat and breath of black tobacco, red wine, and garlic entered my nose. The only sounds were those of a high, crying kite, the swish of the horse's legs through the grass, and the low growling of a gray bull. Over my shoulder, back at the water trough, I could see Fulton pointing something out to Michener, who was nodding his head in agreement.

Gazing across the field at the man in the gray trousers and windbreaker, I reflected on his fame as an author and his non-identity as a public figure. Among the millions of persons who purchased his books, certainly many readers felt curiosity about Michener the man. However, James A. Michener had chosen not to become public property. He lived his life in privacy and behaved in such a manner, in spite of three marriages, that his normality made him un-newsworthy. He didn't drink heavily and commit adultery or he hadn't become a dilettante–he was just who he was before he had become famous and he stayed that way. Throughout the course of my friendship with him, which started that spring of 1961, I tried to remain as objective as possible in my assessment of Michener the writer, something that isn't always easy with such a close and famous friend for a working partner. Often throughout the years I admitted to myself that if I hadn't met Michener in Sevilla or weren't on a trans-Atlantic flight with nothing else to read, I would never have picked up one of his books.

Later that afternoon, as we left Diego at the ranch house and began walking rapidly along the muddy road towards the car, a flock of swallows darted low over the rice fields and glided inches from our feet, snatching insects flushed by our moving legs. We quickened our pace, for the wind suddenly dropped, the air hung heavy and the darkening sky indicated rain was about to fall. Camera slung over my shoulder, trailing behind Michener and Fulton, who were talking about Mexico, my thoughts returned to the bull book. Just then, probably set off by the ion-filled air that precedes a storm and which seems to so excite fighting bulls, one of the great beasts in the field behind us began to roar, and before my friends had a chance to stop and turn around, I curved my arms out in the position of a set of horns, stiffened my forefingers and jabbed them into the broadest of the two backsides in front of me. Jumping forward as his head swung around, "Damn you, Vavra!" shouted Michener as he roared with laughter.

We quickened our step as the first raindrops splashed the muddy road, and within seconds the fields of rice on either side of us grayed as the cloudburst struck. Even though the car was still only a black speck in the distance, we couldn't run because of the slippery mud. Instead, we continued on as fast as we could with our jackets pulled over our heads.

We had walked about ten minutes when, above the sound of the storm thrashing the rice paddies and of the sloshing of our own feet, I thought I heard a child crying. Suddenly, both Fulton and Michener stopped in front of me and turned around. I also looked back over my shoulder into the wind and rain. Running towards us, completely naked and screaming like a wounded coyote, was a gypsy boy who must have been five or six years old. Where he had come from, we never learned. While John knelt down and tried to comfort the boy and find out where he was going, Jim Michener, his high forehead glistening and his glasses blurred with rain, removed his gray windbreaker, knelt down, and hooded it over the child's head and shoulders.

As rice shoots in the paddies behind my friends were doubled and bent to the water by the strong wind and as the gypsy child looked up with grateful almond eyes at the man who hovered over him, at last I saw Michener in a role that could be identified with the books he wrote. Without tattoos, without a captain's cap, there was James A. Michener, the American abroad, acting out a scene of kindness and compassion that had as its background a setting that could hardly have appeared more oriental. Caught up within this small drama, oblivious to the storm, it wouldn't have surprised me a bit just then if Michener, as he rose to his feet and patted the boy on the head, had bade him goodbye with "*Sayonara*."

Reaching the Ford Consul, we discovered thick mud already oozing around its smoothly-worn tires. We put the small gypsy boy inside the car while the three of us, completely soaked, pushed for three or four hundred feet until our footing became firmer. Another quarter of a mile down the road, as we neared a thatch-roofed shack, our small companion motioned that this was his destination, so we left him there, Michener's jacket still around his head, and continued on our way.

That same evening, after we had all warmed ourselves with hot showers and changed into dry clothes, we met at El Meson, a little restaurant behind the post office. There, over *huevos a la flamenca*–a hot casserole dish of eggs, vegetables and sausages- we discussed the day's adventures, along with the Concha y Sierra family history, as John Fulton offered anecdotes of the ranch's present owners. When we had finished our meal, John, Ileene and I walked with Jim along the rain-slicked streets towards the cathedral which was next to the Arab palace or Alcazar.

Those were the days before the Giralda tower was tarted up with floodlights. And so, as we arrived at the cathedral and looked up, the tower tiles were shimmering like the scales of an underwater iguana, illuminated by a moon that appeared and disappeared from low-moving storm clouds. While we leaned back against the wall of the Arab palace, Michener, in his deep voice, began retracing for us the Moorish occupation of Sevilla. He did so in such a way that between the beauty of the romantic scene before us and the words of the night's narrator, we stood looking up as if in a trance, so much so that when the story ended, I had the sensation of being awakened from a dream. How long we had remained there, I don't know, though it must have been almost an hour. This was just one of scores of times that I would spend with Jim in which his commentary on historic events and happenings intertwined with a present-day scene, would hold me and everyone in our company fascinated. Being with him on such occasions was like having a reading from one of his books, hearing words about Arab princes and wars while feeling behind our backs the rough surface of stones carved and lifted by Arab hands as the scent of jasmine, possibly from the distant relatives of plants tended by Arab fingers, made us heady. If history didn't make sense to us after being with James Michener on such an occasion, it never would.

When John and Ileene left Jim and me at the cathedral, I was glad, for I had wanted to be alone with him. After our day with the bulls in the marshes, this seemed like the right time to mention the foreword to the bull book. It was an uncomfortable moment, knowing that Michener and other famous artists are forever being propositioned for their time. Finally, as we walked along the narrow street towards his hotel and were casually talking about plans for spending the next morning at the corrals near Sevilla studying the bulls that were to be fought in the spring fair, did I nervously mention the foreword to my book. Answering in a very matter-of-fact way, as if there was nothing unusual about my request, Michener told me he liked what he had seen of the book, he thought it would be a valuable document, and that he would be glad to write a few pages for it. Not yet having had anything serious published, I was overjoyed as I left the Alfonso XIII Hotel and walked alone back towards the studio with the new confidence that an author of Michener's reputation was willing to spend some of his words on what would become *Bulls of Iberia*.

In the days before the fair started, I would pick Jim up every morning in front of his hotel and we would drive to the corrals of the Venta Antequera, where the bulls for the *corridas* were kept. There we would stay until lunchtime. After having spent almost two years studying fighting bulls in the marshes of the Guadalquivir, I had by this time acquired a certain amount of insight into bull psychology and into the social order within the herd. At first, Michener was amazed at my ability to predict an animal's performance in the ring judged on its behavior in the corral. However, my predictions were based on simple signs read from the response of brave cattle to the corral situation. If a bull charged around the enclosure, sent into a rage by the slightest movement, or if he pawed the ground continually, the chances were good that he would show himself to be cowardly in the bullring. His aggressive action in the corral could be read as insecurity. The animal that is calm and quiet in the enclosure, secure within himself unless separated from the herd and faced with true threat, usually performs bravely in the ring.

Michener learned rapidly about fighting bulls, and by the time we had spent several mornings at the corrals, he could predict with a startling degree of accuracy how an animal would respond in the ring. Following the first few days, during which I instructed him at the corrals, we would arrive at the Venta Antequera and separate until it was time to leave for lunch. The hours that each of us spent alone were devoted to intently observing, while making extensive notes on the animals that were to be fought and killed that afternoon.

During lunch we would compare our notes, after which we anxiously awaited the *corrida* that would determine which one of us had been more perceptive. Since I was sitting high up in the bullring's cheap seats and Michener down in the third row expensive section, we had to signal back and forth to one another with unsophisticated arm-waving, thumbing our noses at each other or clenching our hands overhead in signs of victory, depending upon which of our bull predictions had been most accurate.

It was during the fair that Michener's wife, Mari, arrived in Sevilla. Since we knew that Mrs. Michener was Japanese-American, I must admit we expected something like the tall, exotic dancer heroine of *Sayonara* to walk into the Alfonso XIII Hotel lobby that bright spring afternoon. Instead, however, we saw a short, ordinary, but attractive in a pert sort of way, Japanese woman coming to greet us.

During those days of the 1961 Sevilla fair, I observed in Mari Michener a strange combination of American female independence and aggressiveness combined with feminine Japanese submissiveness. Mrs. Michener's life was her husband, and he gave her an almost free rein in arranging his social program. She was extremely protective and defensive of Jim's time and work; yet there was also a certain amount of independence in their relationship. Often Michener would be working in different parts of the world, leaving Mari in Madrid, Paris, or at their Pennsylvania home in Bucks County. How she busied herself during those hours and days I don't know, though she was meticulous about everything she did–sometimes almost overly so.

Though Mari was strong-minded and could be stubborn, even with Michener, it was clear after the first hours we spent with them that his word was final. If she protested about being left at home, I'm sure she met with the same response from her husband I heard on our first night out together at the Sevilla fair. By the time we had eaten and walked around the fairgrounds, it was after midnight. For us the night had just begun–we knew some gypsies who were organizing a party that would last until dawn at one of the *casetas*—and so when Mari said, "Come on now, Cookie. It's late and we have a big day tomorrow. Let's go back to the hotel." Michener smiled, but in a very caring way, and replied, "Well then, Cookie. I think we'll find you a cab and you can go back to the hotel and get some sleep. There's a gypsy flamenco singer that we want to hear tonight." Though an expression of slight protest could be read from Mari's face, her departing words were, "Now, Cookie, don't be too late," as we put her into the taxi cab.

The use of affectionate nicknames is relative, natural to those who invent them, and often trying and artificial to outsiders. I could not bring myself to call Hemingway "Papa." I addressed him as "Ernest." The use of "Cookie" by both of the Micheners also seemed strange at first to my ears, but after I had spent a week with them, it sounded natural. Perhaps if I had spent more time with Hemingway, "Papa" would also have been okay.

The week went so fast that soon it was time for the Micheners to leave Sevilla, which, after the fair, returned to its normal pace. From Andalucía Jim and Mari flew to Madrid and the important San Isidro Fair. As long as they were in Spain, though, we kept in touch by postcard or telephone. Before Jim left Madrid for America, I received a note from him in an envelope that also contained my hundred-and-fifty-dollar fee for research on the Concha y Sierra ranch. What a joy receiving that check was! Then, in Spain, the peseta exchange was almost seventy to the dollar, and a pair of handmade country boots that today cost three hundred dollars could be purchased for seven hundred pesetas. Because John, Ileene, and I were by then splitting the studio's forty-five-dollar-a-month rent three ways, my check from Michener paid ten months' rent for me. In the years that followed, this plan of sharing expenses with compatible companions living under the same roof would allow me and my friends, generally all down-and-out but hard-working artists, the chance to devote all of our time to our art. We didn't have to take on outside jobs to support ourselves, while at the same time we could enjoy a standard of living, splitting expenses two or three ways, that we could never have afforded alone. By myself I could never have at that time supported a maid. But in those days the old lady who made our beds and cleaned the studio charged only fifteen dollars a month, which made it possible for the three of us, at five dollars per month each, to enjoy this added luxury.

June came, and the Micheners couldn't have been home in Bucks County for very long when John Fulton received a typed, single-spaced, four-page letter from Jim. Unlike other celebrities who had passed through Andalucía, Michener hadn't forgotten his friends in Sevilla! In his letter he wrote of the painting he had commissioned from Fulton, and gave advice on John's career in bullfighting. He wrote of the museums he had visited in Europe and offered his thoughts about Fulton's life as a painter after he had retired as a matador. The many words in that long letter revealed how much he cared for John.

Fulton responded earnestly to Michener's reinstated interest in his career by beginning a series of pen and ink drawings depicting Andalucían bulls, cows and calves in their pastures, while I anxiously awaited for the preface to my bull book to arrive.

Toward the end of June I began to make plans to attend the running of the bulls at the fiesta of San Fermin in Pamplona. Even though there were reports from friends of friends in America that Ernest Hemingway was in the Mayo Clinic for shock treatments, Juanito Quintana wrote me from San Sebastian that he felt Hemingway would be coming to Pamplona. This possibility made my approaching trip especially attractive, for I had recently had the good luck to photograph a range combat to the death between two bulls, after which I had photographed vultures and other birds feeding on the carcass of the loser. I knew that Hemingway or any other naturalist would find the series exciting. Also, since Hemingway had turned me and thousands of other Americans on to San Fermin with *The Sun Also Rises*, the thought of being at the fiesta in his company was thrilling.

June passed and San Fermin drew closer. The fiesta always starts on July 7th and I was planning to leave Sevilla, a two-day drive then from Pamplona, on the 5th. On the morning of July 3rd, having stashed aside several dollars of the Michener money for special occasions, I took fifteen cents of it for tea and croissants and walked down to the Calle Sierpes and the Los Corrals Cafe, where I found Juan Belmonte having coffee. When Belmonte saw me, he motioned for me to join him. Later, as we sat there on that lovely morning, I told him I was going to San Fermin, where I hoped to see Hemingway. Belmonte had been the matador to revolutionize the Spanish national fiesta, the great competitor of Joselito in the golden age of bullfighting, the rival of Hemingway's matador Pedro Romero in *The Sun Also Rises*. He was a marvelous man with a wonderful sense of humor, and as we sat there he told me, "That Hemingway. I never knew anyone to ask so many questions. *Hombre*, why I can remember in Madrid when Cayetano Ordoñez and I would be sitting in the café, and when one of us would see Hemingway enter the door, he'd warn the other and we'd either lean into a newspaper or try in some way to cover our faces, hoping that he wouldn't see us and come over and sit down. Don't get me wrong, he was a nice enough fellow, but he asked so many questions."

Just as Belmonte was finishing his story and I was reflecting on how hard I had searched out Hemingway while Belmonte had avoided him, John Fulton walked towards us. It was unusual to see him at this hour, for he spent most mornings training with other *toreros*. As he drew closer, his face was flushed and there was an unusual tenseness in his manner. "Good morning, Don Juan," he said and then asked Belmonte's permission to sit down. "I'm afraid I have some bad news." He then glanced over at me. "I just heard on the radio that Ernest Hemingway is dead. And although the reports are confusing, it sounds like he shot himself."

Belmonte sighed and pushed himself back in his chair. I sat, stunned. Even though my last impressions of Ernest Hemingway at the Jerez Fair had been so gloomy, I must have secretly hoped that he would be able to shake whatever malady had overcome him. Belmonte did not look at us but stared, as he frequently did, off into the street, watching for someone who never seemed to arrive at his table. Then he folded his hands and, looking over Fulton's shoulder, stuttered, "*B-B-Bien hecho*. Very well done." He then rose from his chair, pulled a hundred-peseta note out of his pocket to pay for our breakfasts and said, "*Adios*. I have to see some bulls in the country," then walked away.

Pamplona was exciting. Though times had obviously changed since *The Sun Also Rises*, still, much of the atmosphere remained, made more colorful by a number of carbon copies of Hemingway characters: "Lady Brett" was a British woman who followed the bulls and was involved in a love affair with John Fulton; "Robert Cohn" was a wealthy Texan who wanted to be a writer but didn't write and hated me because I was at least working at it; and then there was wonderful, warm Juanito Quintana, the real Montoya from the book and the great friend of all of us young aficionados. Though we all danced and drank and went on picnics near Burgette and attended the bullfights every afternoon and at night watched the fireworks in the Plaza Mayor, still there was a certain sadness hanging over the fiesta. The Ernest Hemingway who had introduced us to San Fermin and who in his youth had so enjoyed the people and places and experiences that we were living had somehow gotten off the track. "To get off the track is one of the worst things that can happen to a guy," he had told me in Malaga, "because once you're off, it's damned near impossible to ever get back on again." That's what really hit us: To think that a man who had lived so much and written so well and who seemed so strong, could get far enough off the track to pick up a shotgun and blow out his brains.

Back in Sevilla, by keeping the studio window shutters tightly closed during the daylight hours, we tried to escape the August heat which beat down upon the city with unusual harshness. At night the only way we could sleep was to drag the mattresses of our beds onto the cool tiles. One morning I was still on the floor, having slept late, when I heard the postman call "*Correos*" at the door below, and in a few minutes Ileene's brother Bob, who was then staying with us, was standing over me with a large envelope in his hand. "This is from Michener," he said, letting the envelope fall onto the mattress. I looked at the return address. It was the first correspondence I had had from Jim since he had left Spain. Then the thought penetrated my drowsiness–the envelope was so large that it could only contain one thing, the foreword to my bull book! "Well, aren't you going to open it?" asked Bob.

For a few seconds I sat on the mattress, savoring the expectation of the moment, and then I asked Bob to run down the street to the corner bar for bottles of beer and Serrano ham, cheese, and bread. Before he could protest, I told him that by the time he returned I would be dressed and we would take the envelope out to the Concha y Sierra ranch where it would be opened and its contents read in the proper setting. Obviously amused, for he was a good friend who had known me since we were eight years old, but still slightly aggravated by his part in the game, Bob muttered as he left the room, "You've always been a bloody romantic. Aren't you ever going to grow up?"

Several hours later, as the sun blazed white from a sky specked with buzzards and as a gray Concha y Sierra bull lifted his head to roar, Bob and I sat on the end of a water trough under eucalyptus trees while I anxiously ripped open the envelope from James Michener and began to read the four typewritten pages that concluded:

"It is this mystical quality of the fighting bull, the only truly honorable element in the bullfight–that Robert Vavra has caught in this book. As I said at the beginning, I know of no one else who has the skill and who has spent the hours necessary for the writing of this work. It is thus a very personal document on a subject which has fascinated men for some thirty centuries: Why should one curious breed of animal, the fighting bull of Spain, be the bravest, most dedicated and noblest adversary that man faces in the natural world?"

We stayed at the ranch until the fields began to color with the warmth of closing day, when cattle egrets in white swarms circled around the eucalyptus trees, waiting to roost, and then, with the sounds of a calling bull in my ears and with Michener's words in my mind, I left Concha y Sierra, fortified with the responsibility the four pages of paper I carried in my pocket had given me: To continue working for another five years to finish a book which, although it would be one of my lesser known works, would give me satisfaction for the rest of my life.

After an acknowledgement of my letter of thanks to him for the foreword, we in Sevilla didn't hear from Michener again until after John Fulton made his formal debut in the Las Ventas ring of Madrid. John, who hadn't fought all season, had been trying to arrange a *novillada* in Madrid for years. He had about given up hope when in early October the Las Ventas *impresario* phoned and said, "Be here to fight next Sunday."

Four days before the Madrid *novillada* it had been arranged with a bull breeder for John to fight and kill an animal at a small ranch ring near Sevilla. This would at least give our friend some practice. But the bull was an old, blind-in-one-eye animal that was almost unworkable. The only thing that it provided John with was the chance to practice the kill as he dropped the beast with a superb sword thrust. That same evening, however, it seemed that luck was finally with Fulton when his manager received a call from an *impresario* asking that John substitute an injured matador the following day in El Puerto de Santa Maria.

The next afternoon in El Puerto, Ileene and I sat overjoyed as we watched John give two fine performances. He did so well, killing each of his animals with a single sword thrust, that he was awarded the ear of his second bull and was carried on the shoulders of the happy crowd all the way from the ring to his hotel. The only tense moment during the fight came as the last bull cut in during a right-handed pass and stepped on John's foot.

By the time Ileene and I reached the hotel, Fulton's ankle was swollen twice its normal size. "But it'll be alright tomorrow," everyone confidently assured him.

The following afternoon, Friday, with Madrid just two days away, John Fulton's ankle was as swollen as it had been the day before and even more painful—he couldn't walk on it. Spanish friends came in and out of the studio, mostly bullfight aficionados, and they advised: "Fulton, don't go to Madrid. You can't fight like this."

On Friday night John's condition had not changed when Bob Martin phoned from Madrid. After Ileene had explained the situation in Sevilla, her brother said, "It's just as well, because they'd probably kill him here no matter what he did on Sunday. Now you're not going to believe this, but a couple of days ago some American airmen from the Torrejon Base got so drunk in a bar on the Gran Via they urinated in their empty whisky glasses and then went out on the street and tossed the piss all over some Spanish women who, the rumor has it, were titled ladies. Anyhow, the Spanish government has asked that the airmen be removed from Spain and all Madrid's talking about it and are down on Americans. So, tell John to stay in Sevilla!"

But John did go to Madrid. As the car carrying him and his assistants arrived at the ring, a dozen Spanish mounted policemen formed a passageway for them, holding back the hostile crowd, but not their shouts: "Yankee go home! Let's see if a bull gores you and tosses you into orbit with your countrymen!"

It began to rain as John fought his first bull—adequately well, considering the slippery surface of the ring and that he hadn't been able to walk on his foot for three days. The few good passes he was able to give were met with both *"olés"* of approval and whistles of dissent. John's second bull was the largest of the lot. It was an extremely strong animal with wide-set horns. When the moment came for the picador to pic the bull, the president of that afternoon's fight allowed the animal barely to be scratched before he ordered the horsemen to leave the ring. John, who was then limping noticeably, was left to try to do something with this cowardly but strong bull. At last, when the time came for the kill, Ileene and I looked at each other with relief, for in the past four days Fulton had killed three bulls with a single thrust each.

As John went in over the horns and made his exit off the animal's flank, we could see that he had placed half of the sword in the bull's body and in the proper position. What was happening, we wondered, as his assistants ran out to spin the animal with their capes—a normal procedure in Madrid—but were ordered back to the fence by a police delegate. The bull did not seem bothered by the sword and, not having been weakened by the picador, strongly stood his ground. John removed the sword, entered again and hit bone. Again he lined up the bull, but before he had time to enter, the animal began cowardly pawing the ground and retreating. After that, as the rain fell with more force, John must have entered eight or ten times with the sword. Why he kept trying to go in over the horns instead of stabbing the bull unethically but effectively low in the neck, I don't know. Later he said he had had the foolish idea of having to kill properly because he was in Madrid.

When the bull was still on its feet twelve minutes after Fulton had taken the sword and *muleta* to begin the last part of the fight, the president signalled for the first

"Sincerity is what counts," answered Jim. "There are all kinds of people, and each one receives a different message from a book. The important thing, I guess, is that they read. But God-darned, you meet some charmers. Did you see that great blond dumpling of a woman who asked me if I had Marlon Brando in mind when I wrote *Sayonara*? Them's the ones that makes every evening like tonight a real thriller. Sure, I appreciate all of the sincere straight compliments, but I don't think I could ever get through another one of these sessions if I couldn't look forward to meeting people like dumpling lady. God, how I love them!"

We had left the fairgrounds and were walking along the moat of the university, once the old tobacco factory where Carmen of the opera had supposedly worked. As we neared the hotel, I felt the urge—one that hadn't occupied my thoughts all day—to feel out Michener about a possible book on Spain. The fun of the evening was now suffocated as nervousness overcame me. I took a deep swallow and said, "Smell that jasmine. Spain. What a country."

"Yes, it's a marvelous place," commented Jim as we reached the gate to the Alfonso XIII Hotel. "It's kept me coming back for thirty years."

I cleared my throat. My head was suddenly buzzing. "You know, a great book could be done about this place."

"Oh?" was the only sound that came from Michener.

I was too tense to even look over at him. 'It's now or never,' I thought. "Have you ever considered doing a book about a foreign country and maybe using photographs along with the text?"

We were now on the hotel steps. "Funny you should mention that," he said. My heart was pounding with excitement. "It seems that more photographers have given it thought than I have. Every week Helen Strauss, my agent, receives propositions from photographers suggesting projects to me. Some of them are famous, some unknown. Just before I left, we had a fine offer from Karsh of Canada. You know, he did the Hemingway cover portrait for *Life*. And he put forth his entire negative file with the hope that we could make a book out of it."

Like a bucket of cold water, those words fell on my head. "You fool," I thought to myself, "You were presumptuous. You were stupid to have ever imagined doing a book with Michener. Wake up. You're someone he cares about as much as he cares about the hundreds of young people he's met in cities all over the world. How you can kid yourself?" The note of nervousness in my throat was replaced by hollow disappointment as I said, "Karsh. Boy, it's hard to beat that name. There aren't many photographers that famous."

"Well," continued Michener, "I wrote Helen to tell him 'no.' I've got other things on my mind."

Embarrassed, I reached for conversation, hoping that Michener had not realized what I had tried to suggest to him. "Whatever happened to the Mexico novel? Is it finished?"

"Didn't work out." He put a foot up on one of the hotel steps and rested his weight on it. "But that's part of the game. You can't win them all."

"Yeah, but what about all of your time and research?"

"You just have to chalk that off to a good idea that didn't work out. Before I finish a book, though, or if I start one and it doesn't pan out, I have other ideas, like kettles on a stove, ready to boil over. It's good to keep a number of things brewing in your mind." Then, in what seemed to me as an obvious move to change the conversation, he said, "Instead of doing the corrals tomorrow, why don't we have a picnic in the pine groves at the edge of the *marismas* where you once took me. I mentioned it to Patter and she said she'd pick up most of the food in the morning. Can you meet us here about noon?"

As I left the hotel, my embarrassment and depression mixed with a feeling of warmth for Jim Michener. Of course he had known what I was suggesting, and he had handled the matter in a gentle fashion. But then he was probably used to saying "no" in a nice way to young people with "big" ideas. Anyway, what was wrong with just being friends, even if there was no book? He had thought enough of me to do the foreword for the bull book. Who in their right mind could expect more than that? These and other things I told myself again and again that night, but hard as I tried, I could not quiet my disappointment. "You have to think big," my father had always told me, "or you won't get anywhere." 'But you also have to be realistic,' I told myself. I had learned that from my few years in Spain, even though it was sometimes no fun to be so.

The next morning was the kind of a day that makes Sevilla one of the most wonderful places in the world to be in springtime. As I walked toward the hotel, freshly-opened sycamore leaves formed lime-green stars against the azure sky and the newly arrived swallows, swifts and kestrels pierced the fresh air with mating cries. Patter and Michener, who had been out early, shopping, were just loading the car with boxes of food and drink when I arrived at the hotel.

Not long after we had left Sevilla, we came to the village of Puebla del Rio and drove along the edges of rice fields, the car bumping along the pitted road. As I listened in the back seat, Jim Michener told his wife and the Ashcrafts about our night at the American *caseta*, describing in detail the words and gestures of the blond dumpling lady. Apparently, though, I had not heard her when she had also asked Michener how long it had taken him to write *Mutiny on the Bounty*. "Thank God," I thought to myself, "he's not telling them that Vavra almost had the nerve to suggest Michener and he do a book together."

Before long, we were on the dirt road that leads into the pine forest, and as we drove along, pairs of bee-eaters, having recently returned to Spain from Africa, left their pole fence roosts, soaring and gliding in flashes of yellow and turquoise. Far into the forest, we turned off the main road onto an almost obscure tractor path that I had journeyed over many times. Once within the depths of the pines and with no signs of civilization in sight, we parked the car. When the motor was turned off, the smells of new spring grass and flowers and of the pines themselves delighted our nostrils, while to our ears came that wonderful almost-silence that is so welcome after days spent in the city. Only the soft sounds of gentle surges of wind playing the pine needles in the lofty tops of the trees overhead, not too much unlike the murmur of gentle surf at low tide, and the cries of a pair of black kites that must have had a nest nearby, broke the stillness.

We spread out a horse blanket that Patter, probably with this purpose in mind, always carried in her car, after which we leisurely unloaded the food and drink for our picnic. Although I still felt strong pangs of disappointment from Michener's treatment of my photo book suggestion the night before, at the same time I felt relaxed. Since he had, in his way, rejected the idea, I could forget about it and on this wonderful spring afternoon concern myself with nothing more but enjoying my friends' conversation, along with the beer, Spanish sausages, fresh rolls of bread, Manchego cheese, olives seasoned with garlic, and sardines that were spread out on Patter's horse blanket.

Following lunch, we all stretched out on the blanket or on newspapers and, except when someone remembered a joke to tell, we lay there looking up at the sun moving through the tops of the umbrella pines. Finally Jim got to his feet, threw a small pine cone at me and said, "Do you think we could find that kite nest?"

"Since they're so concerned with us, it must be nearby," I answered.

"Well then, let's leave these sleeping beauties and have a look," he said.

After we had walked about twenty minutes into the grove, with the shadows of the kites more frequently blotting out shafts of light that slid through tree tops onto the forest floor, I spotted the nest in the crown of one of the pines. Not wanting to disturb the parent birds, I turned and said to Jim, "Ready to head back?"

"There's no hurry," he answered. "We still have a couple of hours before the *corrida*. Let's see what's on the other side of that clearing."

After leisurely hiking on for another ten minutes, we crossed the meadow and started up the side of an abrupt ridge. A year before, I had gone up this same hill with my English lover, Vivian. As I climbed higher, I spotted the twisted trunk of an uprooted tree, alongside of which still rested the pile of pine cones that Vivian and I had gathered and then dumped, having decided not to carry them back to Sevilla.

At the crest of that ridge, Jim and I stopped to marvel at the rolling green sea of umbrella pine tops that stretched out before us. Now we were on the same level with the kites and could watch as they slid and rose on thermal currents, hovering above the carpet of pines, sailing on stationary wings. Jim stretched out on the grass, took off his glasses, folded his hands behind his head and let the sun fall warm on his face. Still standing, I could see twenty feet up the ridge where the dry weeds from last year were still bent and broken to form a hollow where Vivian and I had lain naked to feel the delicious warmth of this same Spanish sun, inhaled the smell of the pines and flowers, and heard the murmur of the wind through the trees, punctuated now and then by the cry of a kite.

"You're right, what you said last night. Spain's a marvelous country." Jim's words interrupted my thoughts and I walked over and flopped out on the grass beside him. "You know, *Roberto*, last night I told you I turned down that offer by Karsh. Well, I did so because I had another book on my mind, a book that I've been thinking about for the last four years, since I used to come to the studio-remember?-and would sit and look at your pictures." He paused, and every sound suddenly became so acute that it seemed I could hear each pine needle being played by the breeze. "Well, I've had a book in mind since then, but I couldn't say anything to you about it because there were other books. Anything could have happened–I had to go to Israel for that lengthy period of time–and I didn't want you to be disappointed."

As it had done a year ago on this same ridge, but now for different reason, my heart pounded in my ears.

"Bob, I want to propose that we do a book together. Right now let's just title it *A Year in Spain*."

I felt I had to shake myself out of some cruel anxiety dream, but I blinked into the sun. I wasn't asleep!

"We share many of the same interests, and while I know you don't care much about politics and other themes that concern me, I'm sure your emotional reaction to the marks those processes have left on Spain will be pretty close to what mine is. I'm going to give you about twelve chapter headings and I want you to go to those places in Spain and take about 100 of the best photographs that you're capable of producing. I'm not going to suggest specific photographs or influence you in any way, for that would destroy my purpose. We're to work completely independently of one another. But what you do–what we do–has to be damn good, for I'm going out on a limb on this book. As I'm sure you can understand, and their reaction couldn't be more natural, my agent and my publisher are going to hit the ceiling when they hear about this. Naturally, their business is to make money, and it may be hard for them to understand that when I could spend this time doing a novel which would be an almost certain film sale, I'm going to take three years off and collaborate with an unknown photographer on a book about Spain."

My excitement had turned from nervousness to the kind of excitement that is generated by creative thought. As Jim spoke, I already began imagining the book and certain photographs for it.

"Your fee will be one thousand dollars, which may not seem like much to you, but that's what it is. If the book does well, I'll see to it that you earn more. But more than anything, I think this book could provide a handsome showcase for your work, something that would be seen by many people and that could be of immeasurable help to your career." And then, in his abrupt Michener way, which was just as sudden and short as one of his goodnight partings, he said, "Well, we have to get back for the *corrida*."

"Good God," I thought. "How can this guy lay what he's laid on me and then turn it off like a light switch?" But all of the way back down the hill and to the clearing, I asked him questions. "Then it will be this size? Then for the part on Pamplona I'll do this? Then I'll start right after you leave Spain in May and work right through the summer on it? Then . . . ? Then . . . Then . . . ?"

When we arrived at the far side of the clearing and were walking along an almost hidden stream, I didn't finish one of my questions, but grabbed Michener by the arm and pulled him into tall grass next to me. Suddenly the book and my questions about it were forgotten. Parting the grass slightly, I pointed to what appeared to be a small yellow and black orange-stemmed leaf darting back and forth on the stream's surface which was rippled light gold by late afternoon sunlight. Suddenly another form appeared and another, until there were six downy mallard ducklings, followed by their mother, diving and dipping in the water. "Hatched early," I whispered to Jim, who, in his customary way of acknowledgement, lifted his eyebrows until the wrinkles formed tightly on his forehead, at the same time slightly nodding his chin affirmatively.

For the next ten minutes, we watched the mallard family until they swam upstream, and we were just rising up from the grass when–this time–it was Jim who put his hand on my shoulder, gesturing for me to be alert. I watched his eyes searching a break in the pine trees over the stream, and then I heard the high purring cry of a bee-eater. We continued on through the grass, halfway doubled or completely on our knees, until we came to a bend in the stream where flood waters had cut deeply into the soft earth to leave the bank exceptionally high on the far side. And there, flashing back and forth, backlit against a stand of tall, dry weeds, were a half dozen bee-eaters. Several of the birds were busy digging tunnels high on the face of the sandy bank, burrows in which they would nest and which would extend eight to ten feet into the earth. As they kicked and clawed like small frenzied wind-up toys, particles of sand were thrust into the air to fall in silver galaxies onto the surface of the slow-moving water.

When we left the birds and continued back towards the picnic site, I again questioned Michener with book ideas as he smiled now and then, nodding his head under my enthusiastic bombardment. Finally, the voices of Patter and Squirrel, along with Mari's laughter, drifted through the grove and soon the picnic blanket was in sight. It was then that I asked Jim, "Is the book a secret? Is it okay to mention it?"

"Just be discreet," he advised, sensing my anxiousness.

It was Patter, as the others were packing what was left of the picnic into the car, who called me over to where she was gathering minute wild flowers and asked, "I've never seen anyone with such a smile. What were you and Mitch talking about? You sure were gone a long time."

I couldn't think of anyone nicer and with whom I would rather share my good fortune. "Jim and I are going to be doing a book on Spain together." I could feel the smile pulling at the edges of my face. "You're the first to know."

Patter looked at me for a minute, small bright blue eyes sparkling behind her glasses, and then took one of the delicate yellow flowers, stuck it in my button hole and said, "Well, that's just dandy."

And with the placement of that small blossom sunburst in my shirt, one of the great adventures in a life that would be full of adventures was about to begin.

AFTERWORD

"That's not James Michener! You can't use that photo on the cover of this book!" many people would tell me and Debbie Brothers, Michener's secretary of more than twenty years.

"I can't believe you saw him naked and in the bathtub!"

"I never saw him laugh like that."

"I can't imagine he'd clown around like a little kid. You saw him drink wine and beer?"

These were some of the comments about the pictures in this book. I knew James Michener in a foreign country at a special time in his life and in mine. He was fifty-four and I was twenty-six when we met. I was not someone his age or an employee or a business associate, but a kid, "playmate," buddy, collaborator, and protégé. We spent weeks and months together in Spain working, sightseeing, driving for days, joking, and on it went, together in many different places for the next twenty-five years. Other people undoubtedly knew Michener in ways and in situations that I didn't know him. But I knew him distinctly and intimately, as the cover of this book shows, in which I costumed him as Neptune on a Portuguese beach.

I wonder how many people ever heard someone tell Michener to "fuck off!" I did, and that story I can't resist telling here, for he loved it, and until his death we would laugh at its mention:

One evening, following a *corrida* in Madrid, Fulton and I accompanied Jim and Mari to a party given in their honor by a Spanish-American millionaire. "It should be an interesting crowd. Maybe some good flamenco," Michener said. "And you never can tell what contacts you might make."

Orson Welles, writer Kenneth Tynan, and the famous gypsy matador Gitanillo de Triana were there, talking over drinks in a crowded cabaña surrounded by a garden behind the main house. There were Spanish aristocrats and showgirls and the cream of the jet set foreign community. Michener and his wife looked obviously "square" in this *La Dolce Vita* setting. As the night wore on, the more conservative members of the party began to leave. "Come on, Cookie," Mari took Jim by the hand. "I'm tired after that bullfight. And if you, Fulton and *Roberto* are going to get up early to go to Toledo, we better have an early night."

"*Roberto*, John and I are going to stay a little while longer," said Jim. "Let me get a cab for you and I'll be home shortly."

It seemed like Michener had been gone for hours when he appeared from the garden door. "I had a heck of a time getting a taxi," he explained. "What's going on over there?"

"It's Ava Gardner," I answered. "Let's have a look. But first, let me tell you, things are happening faster than I had ever imagined. There was just a guy here who is with some important American advertising firm. He heard that I'm doing a book with you, and said he can line me up some assignments with magazines that are going to be doing features on Spain this year. What do you think of that?"

Jim nodded. "Well, I'd say that's pretty fast. But I'm sure that this sort of thing will start happening to you. Play them all through. However, you should know that often these projects don't work out. If they sound good, though, give each one of them the damnedest try you can." (Days later I would give it my "damnedest try" until I disappointedly became aware that the advertising executive was more interested in my physique than in my photographs.)

How four years had changed the woman of my dreams. If someone hadn't pointed her out to me, I might have imagined the lady sitting on the floor to be Ava Gardner's older sister. Where were the clear eyes, the delicate, tan face and the willowy body that I had seen rising from a white couch four years ago, a moment that had seemed like yesterday? Now the eyes were puffy and discolored, the complexion pasty white, and even a heavy sweater couldn't hide the roll of fat around Ava Gardner's waist. "God, she's changed," I whispered to Michener.

From midnight until two in the morning, the party evolved into a true Fellini fiesta. While Orson Welles stood talking with Kenneth Tynan, and an old female singer in men's clothing and smoking a cigar a la Edward G. Robinson, belted out flamenco numbers, some of the show girls, "models from Madrid" as they were known, began shedding their clothes and gyrating to the guitar music. I was glad then that Mari had been tired. Jim was sitting on a hassock, clapping his big hands to the rhythm, an immense smile on his face, as one of the girls, then completely naked, dangled her "G" string in front of his nose. Again, I was impressed with Michener's ability to completely adapt himself to the scene and situation, something I had often seen him do in the past, though, from the gleam in his eye, he was now thoroughly enjoying himself. Standing in the background watching and listening, I also was having a good time, even though neither the girls nor anyone else paid attention to me. At this party, being unknown and not rich automatically, made me uninteresting. One of the girls had paired with an effeminate Spanish Count who swayed and twisted, taking the woman's part in the dance. Then the lights were dimmed, causing the figures around us–in the smoky glow–to resemble cavern images.

I needed fresh air, so when I saw Michener and John walking towards the door, I followed and we stepped out into the garden. The moon was still high as we leaned against a wall and talked. It was refreshing to be standing in the spring night with only the muffled sounds of the jazzed-up flamenco to remind us where we were. A few moments passed when two figures, giggling and laughing, ran up the garden path towards the house. It was Ava Gardner and a handsome, young gypsy guitarist. *La Dolce Vita? The Barefoot Contessa*? I picked a jasmine blossom and drew its sweetness to my nostrils.

Beside me, Jim and John remained still, watching the figures enter the house, after which a large bay window was lighted. Then thin white curtains were pulled across the glass, which, because of back lighting from a lamp, silhouetted the room's occupants on the curtain. The gypsy picked up a guitar, and the strains of a lonely and very well-played *solear* drifted like the scent of some mysterious night plant through the garden. The woman raised her arms seductively and moved them from side to side. Again laughter as the music stopped, and Ava Gardner began to slowly undress and kiss the gypsy's chest as he removed his shirt. Then the naked female silhouette moved across the room. Blackness. The bedroom light was switched off.

Returning to the party room, we found many of the guests had either left or had gone to the house. For the next few hours Fulton and I spoke with an old flamenco guitarist from Sevilla, while Michener moved from conversation to conversation among the small groups of people who still remained in the room. Just before six in the morning, he tapped me on the shoulder and said, "If we're supposed to be leaving for Toledo at ten, I should get back to the hotel and try to catch a few hours sleep. Also, you'd better return to where you're staying to get your cameras together and try to catch a few winks."

With the exception of several stragglers standing next to the garden door, there were few people left in the room. Approaching the doorway itself, we found the exit partly blocked by a woman who seemed to be holding herself up by leaning against the wall.

It was Ava Gardner, looking very bothered and staring toward the left wing of the big house. When I reached the door, ahead of Michener, I felt terribly uncomfortable and sadly disillusioned as I tried to smile and mumble "Good night" to the double-chinned, blurry-eyed lady who had once been the queen of my romantic illusions. She, in return, simply looked past me.

"It was nice to have seen you again, Ava," said Jim politely, slightly bowing at the waist, obviously also trying to get past her and out the door. When she did not respond, he repeated, "Yes, it was nice to have seen you again, Ava." He was now almost out of the door, but not quite.

Ava Gardner's eyes, which, in spite of her poor physical condition, were still large and lovely and powerful, opened a bit wider as her stare focused on Michener. Her lovely lips parted and in her dusky voice she said, "Oh, fuck off, Jack!"

Once we were into the night, we laughed until we were finally able to hail a cab several blocks from the house. Inside the car, our laughter continued as we glanced at one another and shared the same thought: James Albert Michener—a Pulitzer Prize winner, inspiration for one of Broadway's most famous musicals, best-selling author, guest of honor at the party we have just left—had been told to "fuck off" by one of Hollywood's most glamorous beauty queens. To the lady at the door, he had been just another "Jack."

As we drove through downtown Madrid, the sun's first rays began to light the city, while across from me in the car Jim's large nose, glasses, and high forehead were silhouetted against the moisture-glazed window. "Plain as a school teacher alongside Hemingway's façade," I thought to myself. "As dull as dishwater when compared to Ava

Gardner's spontaneous performances." And yet, while I had watched those two idols of my youth fade in the sadness of their own existence, James A. Michener had remained unchanged. Hemingway told me that he had loved Africa and Spain because they had not been overrun and spoiled–they were places where you could return after a twenty-year absence and find them exactly as you had left them, and in doing so, once more find your own youth. It was a marvelous experience–and people could affect you in the same way. While Ava Gardner and Hemingway had crumbled with their own prosperity, Michener remained so much the same that each time I met him during the next thirty years, if I shut my eyes, I felt as though we were sitting in John Fulton's studio in the springtime of 1961.

James Michener, for some reason, dropped his guard with me, allowing a look at his very private, protected self. I recall Denver after midnight in his near dark hotel room where I was handing him books to autograph when, without looking up from the page he was signing, he said, "Bob, I'm really glad we're friends." Coming from someone else, this declaration would have hardly been noticed, but from James Michener it almost had the impact of a marriage proposal.

Following the first year we met, upon greeting Jim, I would never shake his hand, but rather exchange *abrazos*, or hugs. Face-to-face he told me–that one time–what I told him many times, "I'm glad we're friends."

IN MICHENER'S WORDS

During the many years of our friendship, Jim Michener sent me almost 200 letters which are now in the James A. Michener Library at the University of Northern Colorado. Of those letters, three are included here to provide the reader with insights into Michener through his previously unpublished words.

Of these three letters, the two longer ones are extended versions of earlier letters he had sent me. The amplified letters are not "ordinary correspondence" in that they were rewritten for the possible inclusion in a book that I was planning to do in the early 1970's. Fortunately, that book was not completed to interfere with this more expanded photo and word Michener portrait:

Pipersville, Penna.
29 November 68

Dear Bob and Van,

I am typing out this note in response to a review that Vavra sent me from Spain and to a surprising conversation regarding Vanderford one night when I was campaigning for Humphrey.

To take the review first. It was a savage attack on the book, on me, and especially on Vavra as an incompetent photographer. (For some reasons the reviewer took special umbrage at the captions to the photographs, but he did grudgingly admit that the book had been very carefully edited insofar as the Spanish words were concerned.)

Well, anyway! On everything I write I get a handful of such reviews and they always come from well-informed young men who imply that they could have written the book better than I wrote it, and the funny part about this charge is that they are invariably right. Every damned one of them could have written some one part of the book better than I did; but the sad fact is they never write the books. I do, and as in the case of this book on Spain, millions of people will go to it over the next forty years for their basic insights into a remarkable part of the world. And the critics, who sit around bars with their feet higher than their heads, will continue to assure their handful of listeners that they could have written twice the book Michener did. They will have good lives and will win many free drinks developing this subject alone, and I do not begrudge them their sunny afternoons of triumph.

They would be astonished, I think, if they could see the hundreds of letters that have piled in from the great scholars around the world assuring me that the book was just the opposite of what Vavra's reviewer said it was. They would be surprised, because they could take any book put out by the great scholar, too, and find justified fault with it, too.

I used to be disturbed by these men but I no longer am. They are an inescapable part of the literary scenc and serve a very good purpose. They make us all try a little bit harder the next time.

I was angry, however, at the attack on Vavra. If this reviewer could only have known how carefully we selected those photographs to get that static quality, how we posed them just so to get a hierarchical effect, how we rejected the precise kind of photo he apparently wanted, he would have been amazed. The more I see this book, when people bring it up to me in strange places all over the world, the more gratified I am that we did decide upon an ancient quality, a lambent quietness which perfectly fitted the text, which also strived for those effects.

As for his blast against the captions, he apparently failed to see that someone had worked very diligently to infuse a kind of fairytale quality into them, and for this I am much indebted to Vavra. Whenever I see one of my captions-there aren't too many-I wish I had cut it and asked Vavra for something . . . more archaic, more static, more way out. Well, it takes a hell of a lot of balanced talent to make a handsome book and I hope our boy finds his when he does his book.

The story for Van. At one of my speeches a very handsome young man about twenty-two came up to me and said, "I am deeply indebtcd to you, Mr. Michener, because the girl I intend to marry was seated in your row coming home on the plane from Spain, and she told me that whereas you were very nice to her, it was your friend, a very handsome, dignified professor with a beard, who put his arm around her and consoled her when she burst into tears of regret at leaving Spain. She said that you were nice, but that the professor was comforting." Yesterday I received out of the blue a letter from the woman president of Strafford College in Danville, Virginia, telling me, "One of our girls, Jan Elvin, sat next to you on a flight from Spain last spring and she has stirred up a lot of interest not only in your books but in having you speak to our student body." I am going to write to her and tell her that whereas I am great for speaking and niceness, it's Vanderford who is strong on the handsomeness and the comfort.

Warmest regards,
(Jim Michener) signature

Pipersville, Penna.
1 September 1969

Dear Bob,

The time seems ripe for me to submit a final report on <u>Iberia</u>.

When I first broached the idea of doing this work I had only the most limited hopes for its acceptance by the general public . . . I assured you that whereas we might not gain a lot of readers we would certainly turn out something respectable, something neither of us would be ashamed of. That was about as far as I was then willing to predict.

The fee I offered you for the photographs was in keeping with my own limited expectation. I believe it was $1,000 with the proviso that "if anything good happened to the project, you'll get more." I warned you that the fee was not magnificent but that it constituted, in my opinion, an honest gamble in that even if the book did poorly, you'd have recovered your costs and would have shown your work to a larger audience than before. I advised you to accept.

It was a good advice, because the Book-of-the-Month Club saw the manuscript and liked it, so we could tear up your old contract and offer you a much better. Also there have been additional dividends and I trust there will be more in the future.

It now looks as if <u>Iberia</u> will be the big surprise of my life. It has caught on to a degree that I would not have imagined four years ago when we were planning it. Thousands of people are reading it that I would never have guessed would want so long and so tedious a work. It is being published in many different languages and is having about the same success in each. In soft-cover versions it will go on and on, and from the things scholars tell me in their letters, it looks as if it would be one of the standard works in Spain for a good many years to come.

I am delighted. I wrote this book with no thought of wide readership, only that it had to be the best possible evocation of a land I had grown to love. I had no intention of its serving as a guide book, only that it report the enthusiasm I have always had for this strange and often violent land. It is in no way complete-many readers have complained about the absence of anything on Segovia and Zaragoza, and I regret not having covered Jaen and Murcia-so that it can't presume to be a summary of Spain, but it is certainly a solid depiction of the Spain I knew over a period of forty years.

I am never a good judge of what I've written, and it is not until my mail begins to build up that I get any true evaluation of what I've done. That was the case with Hawaii and The Source. But when the letters from all parts of the world began to flow in, and I can see for myself what the readers are saying about the book, how they react to it and what they see in it, I begin to get a true estimate. From the letters, which have been voluminous, I believe that I did no more than hit the target I had in mind: Those people who inherently like Spain; but since the target was much bigger than I had anticipated, the sales of the book have been larger than we could have expected. I didn't do anything special. There were just more people interested in it than I knew.

Most gratifying have been the letters from leading scholars. There are some, I am sure, who did not like it and others who felt that no one but a Spaniard should have dared to do such a book. Some of these have taken the trouble to tell me of their disappointment, but the vast majority have written to congratulate me on having produced something they can use with their students to give the latter a true taste of things Spanish. Some of these letters, from great experts like Kenniston, are among the best I've received in my life. Above all else, I prize acceptance from my peers, and some of this correspondence goes way beyond what I was entitled to expect. It is a book we need not be ashamed of.

I think the reviews helped a lot. They brought the book to the attention of readers who normally would have missed it, and I am grateful to those who described the book pretty much as I saw it myself. Edmund Fuller, in the Wall Street Journal, wrote more evocatively about the book than I did about Spain, and a writer appreciates that.

I was saddened by the review you sent me from the <u>New York Times</u>, not because it damned the book but because it was so palpably unfair. For a good many years the <u>Times</u> has given books to one man to review, Robert Payne, and consistently he has torn them apart. This I have to live with. I have written some books which have been widely accepted around the world, both by scholars and by the general public, but invariably they start their lives with a negative review from Payne.

As a man who knew us both said, "Payne is better looking than you. He speaks more languages. He has a bigger vocabulary. He knows more important people. He has traveled more, understands more, works harder. He writes about the same subjects as you do, and it just galls him to death to realize that his books are pedestrian and largely ignored while your lesser works go on and on. His reviews always betray his envy and tell more about him than they do about you, but that's all right, because he's a much more important man than you are. It's only his books that are inferior."

I think it's a matter of morality. I think that whenever a man senses a conflict of interest he ought to disqualify himself from passing judgment on the question at hand. I have worked diligently in politics to enforce this rule, and I evaluate judges, legislators, and critics to the nicety with which they observe the rule of self-disqualification. The good ones do it invariably; the poor ones do it never. Feeling as I do about Robert Payne, I could not conceivably agree to write a review of one of his innumerable books covering the same ground I have covered; the principle of self-disqualification would not allow me to do so. I am disappointed that he would not apply the same principle.

I am sorry that <u>Iberia</u> has been an embarrassment to the Spanish government. Some have wanted to ban it outright but others have seen that it is the principal book that travelers to Spain bring with them. So a kind of gray silence has settled upon the matter. The book is not publicly banned, but neither is it publicly available. I understand that if a bookseller imports copies he is quietly visited by the police and advised that it might be better if he did not display them. So he keeps them hidden and quietly disposes of them as best he can, prudently failing to order more.

This is not surprising, and as a matter of fact I judge it to be about what the Spanish government ought to do. The book contains many things difficult for an ardent Spaniard to explain, and it may be best to shunt the whole problem off to one side. I have been told several times that a Spanish version will be printed if I agree to certain deletions required by the censor, and always I have said, "Go ahead." This has enraged my liberal friends who argue, "You should resist them to the death." I rather think that even with deletions the book might do some good in wider circulations throughout Spain, and if the question is ever put to you, you can assure the questioner that I have agreed to a Spanish edition and that it will be forthcoming whenever the censor and I can get together.

My position on this is simple: The original still stands, available every¬where and in various languages, so that if anyone sincerely wants to know what I wrote about a certain topic he can find out. In such a situation censorship affects only a portion and is itself a great deal about the latter.

One thing I will not do. Having agreed to a censored version, I will not then ridicule it or even identify the bowdlerized passages, and I don't want you to do so either, nor any of my friends. This is a contract freely entered into, and it would be grossly unfair of me to castigate it subsequently.

Your photographs have been universally acclaimed. As I anticipated when we started this venture, they added much to the text, and for this I am grateful. They evoke a sense of Spain which is remarkable, and their variation is both rich and surprising. In fact, they could not have been better, and I even doubt whether the use of color would have enhanced it very much.

Several writers have complained that your photographs did not illustrate a specific point I was writing about but seemed to go off on their own. I deem this to be a high praise, because doing the book once more from the start I would allow the same principle. I think illustrations which merely visualize a writer's word are wasted effort, unless the manuscript deals with patents, when a precise visualization might have some merit. What I prize is the photograph which adds to the spiritual concept of the writing, enhances it, enlarges it in its own peculiar way.

Furthermore, I noticed that most of the people who complained about this misspelled words, so that they probably knew no more about writing than they did about photography, and certainly they know nothing about the union of the two.

The best critics praised the photographs for doing exactly what we intended. And I praise them even now for the same reason. I think they ought to get you many additional commissions, because they are very good.

I wish I could convey to you the enthusiasm of the correspondents. They write after a picnic at Roncesvalles, which they see for the first time through what we did in the book. They go to the old stone church at Cebrero and see it in darkness, then write to tell me it remains much as I had seen it. They have a meal at El Meson in Sevilla and report that the cooking is still good. It is this intimacy of contact that means so much to a writer like me, and when he either achieves it in his words or inspires it in others, he is amply rewarded.

One thing surprises me. I thought one of the best parts of the book was that dealing with the demon pastry cook. Really, this is one hell of a story and I thought I handled it moderately well, but not one writer has commented on it, and this distresses me.

What is the passage most referred to? Something I would never guess. It's that bit about the potted partridge at Toledo. Apparently more travelers than I get skizzled by those damned marinated pheasants or whatever they are, because a whole host of people have assured me that they smell just as odiously now as they did then. Who in the world would have expected that such a passage would evoke so much feeling?

But then someone writes to say that because of our book he took side trips to study the Romanesque architecture of the north, or that he sought special permission to visit the bird sanctuary in the south, I am gratified beyond explanation. To help people comprehend is the task of the artist, and when he accomplishes this in a significant area he succeeds enormously. I told him that the last sentence in the chapter on the birds is the best single thing I've ever done, because it anticipated by many years the sudden surge of interest in ecology, a word no one could define when I first used it.

There are many faults in this book, Don Roberto, and if we were doing it over again we would eliminate them. I would cover Segovia, for example, and Jaen. (I always wince when people point out their absence.) I judge that certain critics were right when they complained that I didn't stress adequately the dark terror of Spain. And I regret that I didn't tackle Cervantes, even though at the time I had nothing fresh to say of him; a couple of months' hard work would have enabled me to say something, but I was then too exhausted with other work to find the necessary hours to do the restudy and the reevaluation. I do think, for example, that the time I spent looking afresh at El Greco's masterpiece was more than rewarding, and numerous art experts have testified the same.

My own opinion of the book after this deluge of impression and deep joy of finding it accepted by the people who know, is that by accident we accomplished a minor masterpiece. By this remarkable statement I mean one specific thing.

I think that certain books, almost always by accident, are read by everyone in the world who ought reasonably to read them. The total readership need not be very great, but it has got to be inclusive. Half a century ago a Swiss diplomat came to Japan and found himself laughing at things he saw. He compressed his reactions into a hilarious book titled The Honorable Picnic, one of the funniest books ever written. In talking about Japan I find that people have heard of this book, but in out-of-the way places I find scores of the most unexpected people who know it intimately and who feel about it the way I do. It earns the title minor masterpiece, because everyone who ought to have read it has done so. And the vast others don't matter a damn.

Not long ago a German visited Japan and got mixed up with archery and zen at the same time. Out of this experience he wrote a little book called Zen and the Art of Archery, and maybe the man down the street hasn't heard of it, but everyone in the world who ought to have read it has done so. It has become a minor masterpiece because it is so widely cherished by those who know.

I believe that at the end of forty years everyone in the world who reasonably ought to have read our book on Spain will have done so. And then someone better will come along and give us a new interpretation, with better words and better illustrations, but to do this he will have to have worked as hard as we worked, and he will have to have loved Spain as much as we did, for there is no other way to achieve a minor masterpiece. As for those who will not have read the book, or not liked it, or not understood it, to hell with them for we never had them as targets in the first place.

Congenially,
(Jim Michener) signature

Pipersville, Penna.
30 September 1972

Dear Vavra,

The enclosed check is for John Fulton. With it he should buy that old etching press in Ronda.

I would like to see him do this because with it he could vary considerably the types of art work he is producing. Etching, drypoint, types of engraving and imaginative combinations of black and white and color become available, and I would judge that these are all forms in which he could do much good work. At any rate, he ought to give the process a fling, and if the old press is as good as he says, he would be getting a bargain. But I still can't comprehend what an etching press is doing in a Spanish mountain town like Ronda!

It was refreshing to see that the two galleries you and John opened are doing well. That one is Sevilla is a real gem. You could sell ice cream cones in there and draw crowds. I hope that you two can keep it filled with enough production, and in enough variety, to keep the operation viable. What I saw last week made me think you might be able to swing it. But for God's sake, keep working at it, or the whole thing will gradually decline for lack of inventiveness and application.

I keep going back in my mind to that long discussion of art we had in El Caballo Blanco in Pamplona in 1966 when the whole gang was there. After much kicking around for ideas Bob Daley asked me what my attitude was and I said that I could speak only for writers, but I believed that a man who proposed to take the problem seriously ought to labor like hell–and by that I mean the sacrifice of almost any temporary consolation–in order to get into print that substantial line of books upon which an artistic life for any writer must depend.

Get the damned things into print, even if you have to work all night after a full-time job to do so. Because once they are in existence, things can happen to them. They become eligible for attention, and long after they have been written and edited, they somehow spring to life with a direction of their own. They earn the writer a few extra dollars a year, and when it is all added up there's enough to live on and one has become a professional.

I remember that we kicked this concept around for quite a while, and I forget what we said, but tonight I am more convinced of this basic thesis than I was then. I would like to see fellows like you and Daley and Matt Carney and this talented gal Cynthia Buchanan produce your series of good books, varied, adventurous, experimental, and then watch what happens.

I have always felt that it didn't matter a hell of a lot if one individual book took off and became a best seller or a spectacular one-shot. That seems to me to be in the lap of the gods and there isn't much one can do himself to affect the outcome. In fact, I've seen three extremely able writers destroyed by exactly such a process. They wrote first novels, saw them skyrocket to extraordinary fame, and then had to face coldly the problem of what to write next that wouldn't be a vast disappointment. Two of these young men, Tom Heggen and Ross Lockridge, committed suicide. I won't name the third, a carbon-copy duplicate of the first two, because he is still living. It would have been much better for each of the three if his first book had been a modest success upon which he could logically build.

But if the row of books is in being-and here I mean a series of books such as Dostoyevsky and Thackeray produced among the classics, Saul Bellow and Bernard Malamud among the contemporaries-one's reputation grows slowly but surely and as I said, "things begin to happen." Long after publication someone will want to use a book in a new way or print selections from it, or convert it into a play or a television special, or use it as a basis for some new work. Or people venturing into some totally unrelated area will want to involve you in their project. Or some imaginative magazine editor in Germany or France will have a bright idea requiring your help. Or an edition for the blind will be needed. Or someone quite unforeseen will see in our work the basis for some intellectual adventure also unforeseen.

That's why I am always so eager for young writers to get the work done, for this alone makes them eligible for the great good things that sometimes happen to the creative person. I have watched again and again as some solid artist plugged away in seeming obscurity, unaware that those who would ultimately help him were watching carefully. I would a dozen times rather have a life like that-which is really the kind of life I've had–than to have known some spectacular beginning followed by an agonizing decline and surrender.

So get the work done now. I believe that with your excellent children's books and the very fine things you are doing in black-and-white photography in your bigger books that you will certainly establish yourself as a real professional in several fields and that as your work proceeds various unexpected rewards will flow from it. Because you are certainly making yourself eligible. And that's why I have always been so willing to help where I could.

You asked about critical reception. Don't worry too much about it. Three experiences of mine illustrate the problem, and you can take whatever consolation you like from them.

On the first Monday morning in May in 1948 I received before breakfast a special delivery letter from Carl Brandt, the most powerful and most successful literary agent in New York. I looked at the envelope with considerable apprehension, because some months ago Brandt had rather regally accepted me into his stable, but I was aware that things were not going too well between us.

He was a powerhouse, immensely secure in his own judgments and convinced that he knew how to lead even the most modest talent along into paths of productiveness. At that time he had the most glittering array of talent in the writing business, and he handled it in imperial style. In fact, he quite overwhelmed me, giving me ideas that I could not digest and plans that I did not have the talent to fulfill. I sensed that he was suspicious of my approach and doubtful of my accomplishment, but he used to summon me to his palatial quarters and give me what help he could.

I supposed that the letter brought me bad news, for, if it had been good, I am sure he would have phoned me, so I opened the envelope gingerly and found that I was right. Carl Brandt, dean of the writing business, was telling me that he had studied me for some time and had found me sadly wanting. He was sure that I would never become a successful writer, that I was unwilling to discipline myself when older people were willing to explain what should be done, and that I obviously had no great future. He announced that he was dropping me from his list, because he could not waste his time on young men who showed no promise of ever wanting to write books that the general public would read.

Six hours later on that eventful day, the Pulitzer Prize committee announced that it had chosen me the winner of 1947. The new book on which I had been working with

Brandt would find a publisher-Bennett Cerf-and would ultimately sell several million copies.

A good many years later Virginia Kirkus, who published a confidential report for libraries and bookstore buyers, issued a prepublication review of a novel I had done, The Source. She didn't like the book at all, which was her privilege, but at the end of her review she actually advised librarians not to bother with it because of archaeology, which was rather dull in itself and which I had done nothing to illuminate.

As a result, few libraries had the book on hand when it became something of a success. They had to order hastily, and then to reorder up to twenty and thirty times, because for a period of nearly four years it was the most sought after book in public library fiction.

The point I want to make here is not that Carl Brandt and Virginia Kirkus thought my work was bad; they were professionals and were entitled to their opinion. I have never quarreled with anyone who said he didn't like my writing, because some very good judges have come to that opinion. But when professionals, whose obligations it is to know public taste and the likelihood of general readership, specifically declare that a given book will not be read, they are guilty of an error within their chosen field of competence, and that can be preposterous.

To digress for a moment, some years ago Oliver Statler showed me the manuscript of Japanese Inn, a marvelous evocation of life in old Japan. I read it with keen pleasure and knew it was good, but I felt that it needed more work and said so. Statler was deeply hurt, because he felt that he had polished it as far as he could and that it was ready right now for publication. I told him that if he felt that way to send it to some publisher. He did. The manuscript was accepted as it stood. And it won great critical and popular success, finding place on the New York Times list for better than half a year.

I have learned to take nobody's advice on these matters, because the experts can be so wrong.

Of this I had painful proof when my last novel, The Drifters, was published. A young man in Minneapolis tore the thing apart. He felt that no one my age had any right to deal with the problems of the young, and I judged that he felt he could have written a much better book on the subject if only he had put his mind to it. I didn't object to his literary judgment, because some of it was pertinent. Also it was easy for me to be generous because the book was being avidly sought by numerous foreign publishers who would have a great success with it, because of its timely probing of problems which were becoming universal. In fact, I thought the young man had a pretty good critical eye, and I suspected that if he had written a book on the subject he would probably have turned out a better book than mine.

But then, feeling his oats, he went on to accuse me of deplorable sloppiness in my writing technique. His point was that whereas I used a narrator in the body of my book I had forgotten to use him in the opening chapter. He said something to the effect that in my carelessness I had assumed that no reader would detect this sloppiness, but he had, and other perspective readers would, too.

What were the facts? I had spent the better part of half a year wrestling with the problem of how to introduce my narrator, and at the end of that time I decided that it would be most effective if I permitted him to creep up on the reader. Thus, with the most meticulous plotting, I made no reference at all to him in Chapter One, only slight reference in Chapter Two, more in Three, and so on, constantly revealing more and more about him, until at the conclusion he stood forth-I hoped-in full detail.

Now I don't know whether this is an effective narrative device or not, although scores of trained readers have commented on it favorably. But what I do want to tell you is that I wrote that first chapter three different ways, that Albert Erskine at Random House consulted with me at least four times, that we exchanged letters on the subject, and that I submitted the whole problem to Bert Krantz, the gifted gal who does the final copy editing on my books. In fact, Erskine, Krantz and I held two different meetings to discuss just how this device could be handled for maximum effectiveness, and in the end I had to rewrite all the narrator's appearances.

After all this attention to a detail that would not even concern the average writer, and after all the work involved, to have a bright young man in Minneapolis charge me with oversight was rather amusing. It reminded me again that in this business even the most pompous critic sometimes proves himself an ass.

I give you an even better case, which you are free to pass along to other young writers if you wish. When I submitted the manuscript of my Afghanistan novel to Random House their lawyers quickly saw that I had put myself into a kind of box, from which might emerge a libel suit. The problem was this. The time span of my novel was clearly specified. Now if you say that in 1958 the Japanese ambassador to Afghanistan behaved like a fool, the Japanese diplomat who then occupied the post can sue for libel even though you do not refer to him specifically by name, or even if you call him by some fictitious name. This is simple. There could have been at that time only one Japanese ambassador. Everyone knew who he was. And if you ridicule him improperly, or accuse him of acts he didn't do, you're in trouble.

My specific problem lay with an American embassy official-completely invented and founded on no one specifically-who might possibly be identified with one or more men who served in Afghanistan at the time I was writing. Since our embassy there was small, I could find no way of identifying my character without impinging on the rights of others.

We held editorial meetings and found no solution. Then we called in the lawyers and they had no suggestions. It looked as if I might be forced to drop this character, a rather essential one, and I was unhappy, but finally someone-I believe it was a young man from the law firm-came up with a positively brilliant idea which solved everything. He was looking at a map of Afghanistan and suddenly realized that it had no seacoast, ergo no navy, ergo no naval officers.

"We'll make our man the naval attaché!" he cried. And we did, as happy an invention as I have ever known.

But when the novel appeared one critic had a lot of fun at my expense. He said something like, "Apparently Mr. Michener has never looked at a map of Afghanistan. I have news for him. It has no seacoast, so that the idea of introducing a navel attaché is palpably ridiculous and proves Mr. Michener's lack of attention to detail." Six brave men and Bert Krantz had wrestled with that particular detail for the better part of a month, and the solution they hit upon was positively brilliant.

So don't worry too much about critics. By and large, they give you a fair shake, and I would much rather have a literary ambiente with critics than without them. A perceptive critic for the New York Times, Orville Prescott, practically saved my life, for his splendid review of my first book got me started, and many of the good things which happened to me subsequently can be attributed to him.

Also, a beginning novelist like Cynthia Buchanan, whom I first met dancing on the streets during the Sevilla feria, can be thankful that so many critics hailed her first book,

<u>Maiden</u>, and launched her in magnificent style. If she can build on this, she's off to a great start and can become a figure in the upcoming generation.

But the big thing, Bob, is to get the work done. I have envy and admiration for the person who can do his one superlative book, like <u>Gone with the Wind</u> or some recent sensation which I am sure are one-shots, but I reserve my respect for the tough old professionals like Zola and Tolstoy and Thackeray and Sinclair Lewis and Alberto Moravia and Henry James who slug away year after year, producing the best they can and trusting that when they get that line of books securely on the shelf, something good will happen to them.

I am very excited about Bob Daley's big advance for his book on the New York Police Department. It could prove to be very good, but it is also one more work under the belt. I was overjoyed at the results of Cynthia's first effort and pray that it will be the first of many. And I am reassured by what you've been doing. If you can get the matador book done, and the translation, you will have added good length to your own shelf.

I wish you and John a world of good luck with your ventures, and I do so for two reasons. I believe that any artist is responsible for all artists. We are bonded together, whether we want to be or not. In an inescapable sense, it is us against them. It is terribly difficult to earn a living as a poet, or a sculptor, or a dramatist, or an actor. The world doesn't need what we do, and to wrestle a living from such indifference is a tough assignment. Anyone who succeeds is honor bound to help those who are trying, for we are brothers against the darkness. That's why I read so damned many manuscripts, write so many introductions. It is my obligation.

I am concerned about you and John primarily because you have had the courage to make a major try at being full-time professional artists. I meet too many people who vaguely want to be artists but who are afraid to take that first plunge of commitment. They keep one timorous foot in art and the other safely in business and waste their lives in compromise. Whatever it was they might have done, they do not do. You two have had the courage to make the big gamble and my heart rides with you.

Warmly,

(Jim Michener) signature

In the quarter of a century following the last Michener letter reproduced here, Jim often told me how happy he was that he had chosen an unknown photographer–me–to do the illustrations for *Iberia*. Once was after the publication of my book *Equus* for which he had done the foreword and which apart from being a *Time-Life* major book club selection, would later sell over 370,000 copies in six languages. Michener said that he had taken a chance on having me do the images for *Iberia*. If he felt rewarded, I felt incalculably so for what he and that book would do for my career.

James Michener wanted photographs in Iberia *because he felt pictures are sometimes more effective than words. Sharing those thoughts, instead of writing about our long friendship, the following few pages of images record some happy moments together. And why not start with Jim and the beginning—the photograph of him on this page with William and Mabel Vavra, my parents?*

Sevilla, 1961

Bucks County, 1965

Teruel, 1966

Pamplona, 1966

Pamplona, 1966

Roncesvalles, 1968

Beverly Hills, 1990

Los Angeles, 1992

San Antonio, 1994

Austin, 1996

Everytime I sit down to write anything, no matter how simple, I want to
hit somebody over the head with it. I want to show and illuminate and persuade and
convince. Ikeep it on a very soft pedal and I try not to bore, but I write because I
have burning convictions. I follow two rules. A book about any subject is bound to be
a bad book...and it also fails to convince, so I try never to be too obvious. And although I have never objectivity as my goal, I have a strong desire to be honest. I am
appalled...like to cut my own throat when error is found in what I've done, because
the best persusaion is complete honesty. I do one terrific amount of checking, because
truth is precious, like an uncut diamond.

ACKNOWLEDGEMENTS

Sculptress, naturalist, music lover, muse of artists, patron of the arts, Michener aficionada, alluring, dark-eyed Mexican beauty–Martha Barba would have captured James A. Michener's mind and heart had they ever met.

It is lamentable that such a meeting never occurred when I see Michener's novel *Mexico* placed prominently in the center of Martha's book shelf and at the same time receive a delicious whiff of food cooking from her kitchen. James Michener said many times that he would one day know he was in heaven if Mexican food was served there. Indeed, he would have felt a halo around his head if he had ever sampled from Martha's kitchens the culinary south-of-the-border creations which are served in her homes in California and Mexico.

However, what would have perhaps impressed James Λ. Michener most about Martha Barba–apart from her beauty and talents–is her generosity which is responsible for the publication of this book. "*Olé*, Martha!" he would have shouted, at the same time tossing a bouquet of red carnations to "*esta dulce niña.*"

Debbie Brothers and I met almost a quarter of a century ago in Austin where the Micheners had recently moved and where she would be Jim's secretary until his death. Entrusted with being the exectrux of James Michener's estate, she was instrumental in the publication of this book. During our many phone conversations, Deb's encouragement and valued advice were always appreciated.

Only one example of Deb's mind will provide an indication of the gratitude and affection I feel for her. On the phone she once asked, "Robert, what are you going to use on the cover of the book?"

Without hesitation I replied, "The photo from the title page of Jim walking through a misty forest near Roncesvalles."

There was a pause, and then Deb asked, "Why don't you use that color shot of him when you dressed him as Neptune on a Portuguese Beach?"

"Deb," I reprimanded," you never use a color photograph on the dust jacket of a book of black and white images."

"That's interesting," she answered, "because I'm looking at a color cover on a book of black and white photographs."

"Who would do that?" I countered.

"Well," she giggled. "The book is titled *The Sevilla of Carmen* and it's by some guy by the name of Robert Vavra."

For the many hours spent working with me on this book, restoring the almost fifty-year-old Michener images, I thank my great friend Travis Smith. Once more Travis assisted in bringing yet another of my books to life.

As with the scanning of the images in my last four books, as well as with those in *Michener's the Name*, I express my deepest gratitude to the International Institute of Photographic Arts and the man who founded and directed it, the late Victor Díaz. And my very deepest thanks go to Victor's widow, Martha Barba de Díaz, without whose friendship, trust, and extreme generosity this book would never have been published. Rightly so, *Michener's the Name* is dedicated to Martha. At IIPA I could also like to thank Martha's daughter, Jessica, as well as Lorena Giddens.

For "casting an eye" at the words in these pages and for their valued suggestions, I thank *mi amiga* Joanne Hearst Castro, along with Debbie Brothers, Ron and Gale Vavra, Jayne Parkinson, Mary Daniels, Lynetta Fuqua, and Robert Daley.

Gratitude for the typing of this book's manuscript is first extended to Sally Stein, my wonderful friend and typist for over thirty years. Thanks also go to Sirkka Huovila and to Louise Nielsen.

I am also grateful to The James A. Michener Library at the University of Northern Colorado at Greeley for allowing me to use my negatives and manuscripts which are owned, archived, and copyrighted by them. Special thanks go to Dr. Gary Pitkin.

In Hong Kong at South Sea Press International, I once more thank my friends Frank Ho and George Lo as well as their staff for the splendid job they–once more–have done with one of my books.

Rob Gazdzinsky and Ted Purpero also have my gratitude as does Darrin Pratt at the University Press of Colorado.

PHOTOGRAPH INDEX AND CAPTIONS

ABOUT THE AUTHOR

Robert Vavra's more than thirty books, translated into eight languages, have sold over 3,000,000 copies. Forewards for Vavra's books have been written by James Michener, Prince Bernard of the Netherlands, Sir Yehudi Menuhin, Sir Wilfred Thesiger, Sir Peter Ustinov, Leni Riefenstahl, and Princess Grace of Monaco. His recent documentary, *Such is the Real Nature of Horses*, is presented by Jane Goodall and William Shatner.

Vavra's clients include Max Factor, Roche, Jordache, White Horse Whiskey, Renault, 20th Century Fox, Disney Studios, and Revlon. The Russian Republics used twenty-four Vavra equine images for their national postage stamps.

His photographs have been featured in *Stern*, *Paris Match*, *Bunte*, *Life*, *Playboy*, *Sports Illustrated*, *Newsweek*, and *Geo*.

His film work includes *Lawrence of Arabia*, *Patton*, and *The Horse Whisperer* for which he was a creative advisor for Robert Redford. He also did the film's posters and billboards, as well as having done the cover of the novel upon which *The Horse Whisperer* was based.

Vavra has had over one hundred one-man gallery and museum shows in America and Europe.

Robert Vavra divides his time between his ranch in Spain and the Kenyan Highlands.

Grateful acknowledgement is made to Random House, Inc. for the use of the following photographs from Iberia: *pages 13, 17, 22, 23, 25, 34, 38, 46, 50, 58, 85, and to William Morrow & Co. for the photographs on pages 94, 99, 118, 125, 131.*

Credits: Photographs of James Michener and Robert Vavra (pages 200-202): p.200, top-left - John Fulton; p.200, top-right David Adickes; p.201, top-left - Robert Daley; p.201, top-right - Robert Daley; p.201, bottom-left - Dick Broūn; p.201, bottom-right - Jay Vavra; p.202, top - Donna Parrish; p.202, bottom - Roger Bansemer.